THE BOOK OF
JEWISH VALUES

THE BOOK OF
JEWISH VALUES

LOUIS JACOBS

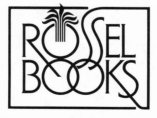

Chappaqua, New York

© Copyright 1960 by Louis Jacobs

Published by
Rossel Books
44 Dunbow Drive
Chappaqua, NY 10514
(914) 238-8954

A *Limited Edition Reprint*, 1983

Cover design and calligraphy by Ann Zaiman

LIBRARY OF CONGRESS CATALOGING IN PUBLICATION DATA

Jacobs, Louis.
    The book of Jewish values.

    (A Limited edition reprint)
    Reprint. Originally published: Hartford, Conn.:
Hartmore House, 1969.
    1. Jewish way of life. 2. Judaism—Essence, genius,
nature. I. Title.
BM723.J3 1983   296.3'85   83-21278
ISBN 0-940646-06-4 (pbk.)

Manufactured in the United States of America

CONTENTS

PREFACE & ACKNOWLEDGMENTS

This attempt at presenting some of the more important Jewish values, with particular reference to their relevance for modern life, is addressed primarily to the general reader. But fairly extensive footnotes are added for the benefit of those who wish to further their studies. For the classical sources of Judaism the standard editions and translations have been used.

*My thanks for permission to quote extracts from various works are due to The Oxford University Press (*THE MIND OF MAN, *by Gilbert Highet, and* THE IDEA OF THE HOLY, *by Rudolph Otto, translated by J. W. Harvey); to Hutchinson and Company (Dean Inge's* THE DIARY OF A DEAN*); to John Murray (John Betjeman's* COLLECTED POEMS*); to the author and to Cassell and Company (Viscount Samuel's* BELIEF AND ACTION*); to Dayan Dr. I. Grunfeld (translator of* JUDAISM ETERNAL—*Selected Essays from the Writings of Samson Raphael Hirsch, published by the Soncino Press); to Mr. Samuel Hertz (Dr. J. H. Hertz's* THE PENTATEUCH AND HAFTORAHS, *published by the Soncino Press); and to Mr. Leonard G. Montefiore, O.B.E. (*A RABBINIC ANTHOLOGY, *by C. G. Montefiore and H. Loewe, published by Macmillan and Company).*

My thanks are also due to the Editorial Board of Judaism, *in which a part of Chapter IV and of Chapter IX first appeared in article form.*

I

INTRODUCTION

THE ideas and ideals set forth in the following pages – the study of the *Torah*, the love and fear of God, the sanctification of the Name, trust in God, holiness, humility, love of neighbour, compassion, truth and peace – are Jewish Values. The use of the adjective is not intended to suggest that these values are the invention, or the exclusive preserve, of Jews; still less that they are not to be found among non-Jews and in faiths other than Judaism. Basic to all the higher religions are ideals corresponding closely to those described as Jewish. Non-religious, as well as religious, ethical thinkers have expounded the worth of humility, truth, love and compassion, but a Jewish value means: (a) that it receives a special kind of emphasis in the Jewish tradition and (b) that it is no remote ideal but a real, vital force in the lives of Jews.

(a) *These values are called Jewish because they receive a special kind of emphasis in the Jewish tradition.*
Take the word *value* itself. It is highly significant that the word *'erekh,* used for 'value' in the later Hebrew literature, originally meant no more than 'estimation' or 'assessment' and was used in the earlier sources for the idea of establishing the monetary worth of an object. In the great formative periods of Bible and Talmud there is no word for 'value' in the sense of abiding or absolute worth: the ancients saw no *value* in value. The genius of Biblical and Talmudic Judaism expressed itself far less in abstract thought patterns and far more in concrete applications. There are very few discussions on the nature of justice and righteousness but there are

constant appeals for justice and righteousness to be realised in the lives of Jews. Holiness as an abstract ideal is seldom defined but there are numerous prescriptions for holy living. In modern theological language, Jewish thinking on these subjects is 'existential' rather than systematic. Similarly, each of the values discussed below is coloured in the Jewish tradition by the typical reactions of Jewish thinkers and teachers who operated within the categories of Judaism. The love and fear of God, for instance, have been variedly interpreted by Jewish teachers but every Jewish interpretation obviously avoids attributing the taking on of human nature by God, as does Christianity, and, on the other hand, refuses to 'depersonalise' the Deity, as in the Far-Eastern religions. With regard to some of the other values, the specific Jewish content is less striking. As we shall see when examining the ideal of Trust in God, for instance, the inevitable tensions between *quietism* and *Pelagianism* are known to Jewish teachers though they are not discussed, of course, under these names. On the whole it is true to say that in each of the values there are sufficient special Jewish insights to permit the use of the adjective.

(b) *These values are called Jewish because they are no remote ideals but vital forces in the lives of Jews.*
All the values discussed here have become so deeply-rooted in the Jewish consciousness that they are generally referred to by their original Hebrew names. To this day it is exceedingly likely that even an ordinary Jew with no pretensions to learning will be familiar with the original Hebrew terms. Thus he will use, or, at least know, the term *limmud ha-Torah* for *Torah* study, *'ahabhath ha-Shem* for the love of God, *yirath shamayim* for the fear of God, *kiddush ha-Shem* for the sanctification of God's name, *bittahon* for trust in God, *kedushah* for holiness, *'anivuth* for humility, *rahamanuth* for compassion, *'ahabhath re'a* (or more commonly *'ahabhath yisrael*) for love of neighbour, *'emeth* for truth, and *shalom* for peace. This not only demonstrates the force of

8

these ideals in Jewish life, but daily use of the terms by the Jew over so long a period has imparted to them a homely character, making them dynamic principles of action rather than abstract academic ideas and suggesting the warm, pulsating life of the market-place rather than the cold, intellectualism of the schools. However, the more rarefied flights of scholars, saints and mystics cannot be neglected and the following pages attempt to convey not only the day-to-day application of the values but as they are found in Jewish literature as a goal for the few.

Although they have received many interpretations, all these are constant in Judaism, and we shall have occasion to examine the particular difficulties of the modern man trying to live by these values. At times these difficulties can be avoided by favouring one ancient interpretation rather than another, but occasionally something more drastic is required such as a completely fresh interpretation. This book is thus addressed chiefly to the reader who finds that the values 'speak' to his situation but that some of their ancient interpretations are unacceptable. This must involve a degree of selectivity, the legitimacy of which might be questioned by some who argue that either Jewish tradition is accepted *in toto* or it is not, and if the right is reserved to select from the tradition, its authority is destroyed by the subjective will as arbiter. But the either-or attitude is naïve and unhistorical. There is no monolithic system of Jewish values but a series of complex applications of Jewish truth in which the more subtle distinctions and shades of meaning were debated at length by the best Jewish intellects. Some selective process is necessary because there are in the traditions many contradictory ideas as well as conceptions which have their origin in conditions no longer obtaining.

This does not mean that we can afford to reject ancient ideas merely because they are inconvenient. It is only an attitude of cynical expediency that justifies the ruthless pruning of challenging ideas by labelling them 'out-moded'. The yardstick to be employed is not that nebulous concept 'modern thought' but Jewish tradition itself. All the same, there *are* problems for moderns, some the result of an outlook owing a great deal to Jewish values themselves demanding a fresh interpretation so that they might be expressed more effectively and with greater relevance to the dilemmas of the present time. We contend that a gap does exist between the values of the past and the spiritual needs of the present but that it is possible to build a strong bridge connecting the two. Those who acknowledge no gap will be irritated by the references to the difficulties of moderns. Those who feel that the gap is unbridgeable will dismiss this book and any other effort as futile. But it is hoped that there are a sufficient number of thinking people who both see the gap and believe that it can be spanned. This book would not claim that it provides even the raw materials necessary for the important task to be carried out; at the most it is a surveyor's estimate of part of the work to be done.

II

THE STUDY OF THE *TORAH*

Elijah Ben Solomon, the Gaon of Vilna (1720-1797), is said to have spent eighteen to twenty hours a day absorbed in his books, allowing nothing to distract him from what he considered to be the highest pursuit of man, the concentrated study of the *Torah*.

'Why is it necessary,' his disciples were asked, 'for your master to spend so much of his time in *Torah* study?' 'If the Gaon studies eighteen hours a day,' they replied, 'the average Polish or Lithuanian Rabbi will study ten hours. If the Polish Rabbi studies ten hours the German Rabbi, in an environment less conducive to such diligent application, will study for six hours, and the English Rabbi for two hours. And if the English Rabbi spends two hours a day in *Torah* study there is a likelihood that his congregants will, at least, keep the Sabbath. But if the Gaon lowers the standard and spends no more than ten hours in *Torah* study, the Polish Rabbi will be content with only six hours, the German Rabbi with two, and the English Rabbi with only half an hour. And if that happens what will become of the Sabbath of English Jews?'[1]

Appreciation of *Torah* study as the greatest of the Jewish values was typical of Eastern European Jewry in the past centuries, of French and German Jewries in the Middle Ages, and of Palestinian and Babylonian Jewries in the Talmudic period. The *Mishnah,* the great Code of Jewish Law, compiled by Rabbi Judah the Prince at the end of the second century, states that of the 'things which have no fixed measure' are deeds of lovingkindness and the study of the *Torah*.[1]

[1] *Pe'ah* I, i.

'These are the things,' the *Mishnah* goes on to teach, 'whose fruits a man enjoys in this world while the capital is laid up for him in the world to come: honouring father and mother, deeds of lovingkindness, making peace between a man and his fellow; and the study of the *Torah* is equal to them all.'[2] Upon which the Vilna Gaon comments that if the study of the *Torah* has no fixed measure then one word of *Torah* falls under the definition of *Torah* study and this one word is 'equal. to them all', more precious in God's eyes than all the other good deeds a man does.[3] The followers of the Gaon were fond of quoting a passage in the *Zohar*, the Bible of the mystics, which in the context refers to mystical knowledge but which was, by them, applied to all *Torah* study[4]:

> How greatly it is incumbent on a man to study the *Torah* day and night! For the Holy One, blessed be He, is attentive to the voice of those who occupy themselves with the *Torah*, and through each fresh discovery made by them in the *Torah* a new heaven is created. Our teachers have told us that at the moment when a man expounds something new in the *Torah*, his utterance ascends before the Holy One, blessed be He, and He takes it up and kisses it and crowns it with seventy crowns of graven and inscribed letters.[5]

The Vilna Gaon's love of *Torah* was inherited by his pupil R. Hayyim of Volozhyn (1749-1821), the founder of the Yeshiba of Volozhyn, the world-famous academy of Jewish learning, to which flocked the studious youth of Russian Jewry in the nineteenth century. Under Naphtali Zevi Judah Berlin (1817-1897), the husband of Hayyim's granddaughter, the Yeshiba reached heights of devotion to learning seldom paralleled. The *Netzibh* (as Berlin was known from the initial

[2] ibid.
[3] Commentary to *Pe'ah* (*Shenoth Elijahu,* in the Warsaw ed. of the *Mishnah*) loc. cit.
[4] See *Ma'aloth Ha-Torah* by Abraham ben Solomon Zalman, brother of the Gaon, Königsberg, 1851, p. 17a-b.
[5] *Zohar* I, 4b.

letters of his name) literally fulfilled the verse in the book of Joshua: 'This book of the law shall not depart out of thy mouth, but thou shalt meditate therein day and night. . . .'[6] After his marriage, for twenty years, Berlin lived the life of a recluse, locked in his room from early morning until late at night engaging in no pursuit other than the study of the *Torah*. On one occasion, at the termination of the long fast day of *Yom Kippur*, his father-in-law, himself a scholar of no mean attainments, was about to recite the *Habhdalah* prayer prior to beginning the meal when it was noticed that Berlin was absent. Search being made for him it was discovered that, oblivious to the pangs of hunger, he was patiently resuming the studies which the day of prayer and fasting had interrupted. Eventually (in 1853) the *Netzibh* was appointed head of the Yeshiba of Volozhyn where the responsibilities of his new position propelled him from his ivory tower to take an active part in the life of Russian Jewry as a distinguished spokesman for Orthodox Judaism and defender of the Jewish faith and people. But the brilliant young men who studied at the Yeshiba were trained in the spirit of austerity and denial in the pursuit of *Torah* wisdom, characteristic of Berlin. Secular learning of any kind was frowned upon, the student of Volozhyn being expected to turn his back on the world, at

---

[6] Josh i. 8. Cf. Men. 99b: 'Ben Damah the son of R. Ishmael's sister once asked R. Ishmael, May one such as I who have studied the whole *Torah* learn Greek wisdom? He read to him the following verse: *This book shall not depart out of thy mouth, but thou shalt meditate therein day and night*. Go find a time that is neither day nor night and learn Greek wisdom.' In the same passage, however, it is stated that this opinion is at variance with the view of R. Samuel b. Nahmani who said in the name of R. Johanan: 'This verse is neither an obligation nor a religious duty but a blessing' i.e. an assurance to Joshua that the book would never depart from his mouth. On the general question of 'Greek wisdom' see the interesting references given in: *A Rabbinic Anthology* by C. G. Montefiore and H. Loewe, Lond., Macmillan, 1938, pp. 145-146.

least for the duration of his stay at the Yeshiba, so as to realise the ancient Rabbinic ideal:

> This is the way of the *Torah*: a morsel of bread with salt thou must eat, and water by measure thou must drink; thou shalt sleep upon the ground, and live a life of pain the while thou toilest in the *Torah*. If thou doest thus, Happy shalt thou be, and it shall be well with thee; happy shalt thou be—in this world, and it shall be well with thee—in the world to come.[7]

For many years groups of students at Volozhyn took turns at studying for hours on end, one group relieving the other, so that at no time of the day or night was the great hall of the Yeshiba silent from echoes of *Torah* learning and discussion.[8]

The Polish and Lithuanian Yeshiboth in the twentieth century conformed more or less to the pattern set by Volozhyn, that of intense *Torah* study cultivated for its own sake as the highest aim of the intelligent Jew. But this pattern had its origin in a far earlier period. Before the common era the Pharisees engaged in *Torah* study and teaching with a zeal and devotion that enabled many of them to defy death rather than forswear their life's work. Psalm one hundred and nineteen (the 'Pharisaic' psalm) is the poet's description of what the *Torah* meant to his people:

> Oh how I love Thy law!
> It is my meditation all the day.
> Thy commandments make me wiser than mine enemies;
> For they are ever with me.
> I have more understanding than all my teachers;
> For Thy testimonies are my meditation.
> I understand more than mine elders,

---

[7] *Baraitha, Kinyan Torah, 'Aboth*, VI, 4.

[8] On the *Netzibh* and Volozhyn see S. J. Fünn, *Keneseth Yisrael*, Vol. 2 (1888) pp. 136-142, Meir Berlin, *Fun Volozhyn bis Yerushalayim*, New York, 1933, J. L. Maimon, *Midde Hodesh Behodesho*, Vol. 2 (Jer. 1956) pp. 49-81, 99-122, Vol. 3 (Jer. 1957) pp. 111-112, S. Sevin, *'Ishim Ve-Shittoth*, Tel-Aviv, 1952, pp. 9-37.

THE STUDY OF THE *TORAH*

Because I have kept Thy precepts.
How sweet are Thy words unto my palate!
Yea, sweeter than honey to my mouth![9]

Many schools of Jewish learning flourished in ancient
Palestine, the best-known being the school at the sea-coast
village of Jabneh which came into especial prominence after
the destruction of the Temple. There were schools at Lydda,
under the guidance of R. Eliezar ben Hyrcanus and R.
Tarphon, at Bene Berak under R. Akiba, at Usha in Galilee,
and at Sepphoris, Tiberias and Ceasarea. The story told in the
little Talmudic treatise, Ethics of the Fathers, is typical of
the Jewish love of learning during the first two centuries of
the present era:

> R. Jose, the son of Kisma, said, I was once walking by the way,
> when a man met me and greeted me, and I returned his greeting.
> He said to me, Rabbi, from what place art thou? I said to him,
> I come from a great city of sages and scribes. He said to me, If
> thou art willing to dwell with us in our place, I will give thee
> a thousand thousand golden dinars and precious stones and
> pearls. I said to him, Wert thou to give me all the silver and gold
> and precious stones and pearls in the world, I would not dwell
> anywhere but in a home of the *Torah*. . . .[10]

'Homes of the *Torah*' rose to a position of importance in
the third century in Babylon, the second great centre of
Jewish life in Talmudic times. At the beginning of this
century two Palestinian trained scholars, Rab and Samuel,
returned to their native Babylon, the former to found the
school at Sura, the latter to revive the long-established school
at Nehardea. When Nehardea was destroyed during the
Roman-Persian wars in the year 259, Samuel's disciple, Judah
b. Ezekiel, founded a college at Pumbeditha which existed as
a sister and rival institution of Sura for over eight centuries.
After the decline of Sura and Pumbeditha in the eleventh
century, new schools sprang up in North Africa and Europe

[9] Ps. cxix, 97-100, 103.
[10] *Baraitha, Kinyan Torah, 'Aboth*, VI, 9.

15

to take their place. The schools of Paris, Troyes, Narbonne, Metz, Worms, Speyer, Altona, Cordova, Barcelona and Toledo were renowned in the Middle Ages. From the sixteenth century, Poland emerged as the Jewish intellectual centre with its own academies. In all these centres the ideal was that of Maimonides, who follows his Talmudic masters:

> Every man in Israel is obliged to study the *Torah*, whether he is firm of body or a sufferer from ill-health, whether a young man or of advanced age with his strength abated. Even a poor man who is supported by charity and who is obliged to beg at doors and even one with a wife and children is obliged to set aside a period for *Torah* study by day and by night, as it is said: Thou shalt meditate therein day and night.[11]

The temptation to idolise and idealise the past must be resisted: not all Jews engaged so assiduously in their studies and the mental horizons of many who did were, at times, exceedingly narrow. Schechter, with some justice, once spoke disparagingly of a number of the Eastern European scholars of his day as 'study-machines'. The numerous references in the literature of Jewish piety about the importance of studying so many hours a day and of the sin of wasting a moment which could be spent in *Torah* study do sometimes suggest an attitude of mind where the act of sitting before the open book and piously mouthing its words mattered more than the mental assimilation of its contents. Nevertheless, it is from the lives of its best representatives that the ideal of *Torah* study should be understood. These men were deeply convinced that the subject of *Torah* study was the word of God and that the student was being afforded the inestimable privilege, as has been said, of 'thinking God's thoughts after Him'. The *Hasidic* leader, Talmudist and mystic, R. Shneor Zalman of Ladi (1747-1812) writes:

> Behold with regard to every kind of intellectual perception, when one understands and grasps an idea in his mind the mind seizes the idea and encompasses it in thought so that the idea is

[11] *Yad, Hil. Talmud Torah*, Chapter I, 8.

held, surrounded and enclosed in the mind in which it is comprehended. Conversely the mind is clothed by an idea which it has grasped. For instance, when one understands fully a rule found in the *Mishnah* or the *Gemara* his mind seizes the rule and encompasses it and, at the same time, the mind is encompassed by the rule. Now, behold, this rule is the wisdom and will of the Holy One, blessed be He, for it rose in His will that, for instance, when *A* pleads thus and *B* thus the rule will be thus. And even if, in fact, a case of this kind will never come before the courts, nonetheless, seeing that it rose in the will and wisdom of the Holy One, blessed be He, that this is the rule it follows that when a man knows and grasps with his mind this rule in accordance with the decision laid down in the *Mishnah* or the *Gemara* or the Codes he grasps, seizes hold of, and encompasses in his mind the will and wisdom of the Holy One, blessed be He, of whom no thought can conceive. (Not the will and wisdom in themselves but as they are enveloped in the rules set down for us.) In addition man's mind is encompassed by them, a wondrous unification than which there is none to compare in material things, to be completely united and actually at one from every aspect. This is the superior virtue, greater and more wonderful in every way, that the duty of *Torah* study and *Torah* understanding possesses over all religious duties performed by deeds, even over those performed by speech (and even over the duty of *Torah* study with speech alone). For as a result of the performance of all the duties of speech and deed the Holy One, blessed be He, clothes the soul and surrounds it from head to foot with the light of the Lord. But with regard to the knowledge of the *Torah*, apart from the fact that the mind is clothed with the wisdom of the Lord, that wisdom is in the mind through the effort of grasping by the intelligence that which each man can grasp according to his perception and the degree of his knowledge. . . . Seeing that through the knowledge of the *Torah* man's soul and mind encompasses the *Torah* and are in turn encompassed by it, the *Torah* is called the food and sustenance of the soul. For just as material food sustains the body it enters and is transformed in the body into flesh and blood by virtue of which man lives and endures, so it is with regard to knowledge of the *Torah* and its comprehension by he who studies with concentration until the *Torah* is grasped by the mind and becomes united with it. . . .[12]

[12] *Tanya*, Vilna, 1930, *Likkute 'Amarim*, Chapter V, pp. 17-19, cf. *Kunteros 'Aharon*, pp. 318-321.

This is a a mystical exposition of an idea present in somewhat similar form in the mind of all the great traditional devotees of *Torah* study. The *Torah* reflects the mind and will of the Deity. Therefore, there can be no higher or more noble pursuit for man than to attempt to encompass the divine will through the diligent study of the *Torah*.

Although Judaism has been described as a religion of action it is important to realise that this is only true of Rabbinic Judaism if action is understood as embracing the operations of the mind. The definition would be correct if it means that Judaism is less concerned with the affirmation of religious beliefs than with the expression given to those beliefs in human life. But such expression is possible in the activities of the mind. The definition is false if it means that Judaism is chiefly interested in the deeds of the human body. The study of the *Torah* is a great end in itself not only a means to practice.[13] The old Jewish ideal of 'we will do' coming before 'we will hear'[14] was interpreted by a latter-day scholar, in the spirit of Rabbinic teaching on this subject, to yield the thought that even after the requisite degree of knowledge has been obtained to enable man 'to do' there still rests upon him the obligation 'to hear'.[15] To understand the *Torah* is an obligation in its own right, apart from the consequences of such understanding in the deed. Gilbert Highet, discussing the faith of Western Universities, is right to describe it as follows:

It is good that we should learn more about the universe and

[13] Cf. Kidd. 40b: 'R. Tarfon and the Elders were once reclining in the upper storey of Nithza's house in Lydda, when this question was raised before them: Is study greater or practice? R. Tarfon answered, saying: Practice is greater. R. Akiba answered, saying: Study is greater, *for it leads to practice*. Then they all answered and said: Study is greater, for it leads to action.'

[14] See Ex. xxiv, 7 and Sabb. 88a.

[15] See S. Sevin: *Le-'or Ha-Halakhah*, Jer. 1946, p. 161, the whole of this chapter in Sevin's book is exceedingly valuable for an assessment of the role of *Torah* study in Jewish tradition.

about ourselves, even although no other benefit than our knowledge ever accrues to us and our fellow creatures. Knowledge is
better than ignorance, even if that knowledge produces no further
results. The man who understands the structure of a distant star-
system, the man who finds an equation to describe the growth
of a leaf, and the man who reveals a forgotten era of history need
no further justification: their work may never be 'used'; it will
still be good. Some of the discoveries made in recent research
have in fact been put to uses that many wise men think evil. The
discoveries remain good.[16]

Most Western thinkers would agree with Highet. Certainly
he is right in stating this as the faith of Western Universities.
And this is, too, precisely the attitude of the classical
Rabbinist, with the addition that for him the ideal is not
alone knowledge for its own sake but *Torah* for its own sake.
The knowledge of God's will arrived at after a severe process
of mental effort is the supreme good.

What were the subjects of *Torah* study? In Talmudic times
Jewish learning was divided into two branches (1) of
Halakhah (from a root meaning 'to walk'), the legal side of
Judaism, its detailed discussions, rules and regulations gov-
erning Jewish life in all its complexity and (2) *Aggada* (from
a root meaning 'to tell'), the non-legal aspects of Jewish life,
the philosophy, ethics, folk-lore, history, Biblical exegesis and
exposition by generations of teachers. There can be no doubt
that pride of place was generally given to the hard *Halakhic*
discipline. The gifted scholar in Talmudic times in mediaeval France and Germany, in sixteenth century Poland and
seventeenth and eighteenth century Russia, Lithuania and
Hungary, devoted his chief energies to *Halakhic* studies.
There is the revealing story of two Talmudic Rabbis, one of
whom specialised in the popular *Aggada,* the other in the less
popular *Halakhah.* The former compared his province to
cheap tinsel goods, which all can afford to buy, but the province of his friend to precious stones for the connoisseur.[17]

[16] *The Mind of Man*, O.U.P. 1954, p. 78.
[17] Sot. 40a

'From the day the Temple was destroyed the Holy One, blessed be He, has no place in His world apart from the four cubits of the *Halakhah*,'[18] is a typical Rabbinic statement.

It has frequently been suggested that this emphasis on *Halakhic* study stifled the imagination and that *Halakhic* subjects were dry and uninteresting, but no student with first-hand acquaintance of *Halakhah* could be guilty of such mis-representation. Naturally, much depended on the type of student. The superficial dipper into *Halakhic* literature no doubt found the subject boring. But as Chesterton said of the expression 'as dull as ditch-water' the naturalist finds the examination of ditch-water a fascinating occupation. The facts are that some of the keenest minds in Jewry found delight in the *Halakhic* dialectics, in the swift thrust and parry of *Halakhic* debate, in the acute analysis of subtle legal concepts, even in the ingenuities of the much-decried *pilpul* (the word means 'pepper', hence a 'peppery argument').[19] Kaufmann Kohler, the well-known Reform leader, ridicules, in his personal reminiscences,[20] this 'problem' set by his Orthodox teacher, Jacob Ettlinger. The Rabbis rule that the 'four species' of plant taken in the hand and waved on the festival of Tabernacles[21] have to be taken 'in the manner they grow on the tree',[22] that is, the right way up. Ettlinger discusses whether they are to be held upside down in the American hemisphere because this is the direction in which they grow on their native soil! Kohler is insensitive to the element of delightful surprise in Ettlinger's problem, to the attempt at working out a novel illustration of how an abstract principle applies in a concrete situation. One might just as well treat as absurd the ingenious speculations of the ancient mathematicians as to whether Achilles can succeed in his

[18] Ber. 8a.
[19] See article *Pilpul* in J. E. Vol. X, p. 39f.
[20] *Studies, Addresses and Personal Papers*, New York, 1931, p. 474.
[21] Lev. xxiii, 40.
[22] Sukk. 45b.

race with the tortoise.[23] This lack of *Halakhic* appreciation
is also evident in C. G. Montefiore's introduction to the
valuable *A Rabbinic Anthology*.[24] Montefiore writes:[25]

> This total omission of Halakhah from my book, though unavoid-
> able, must, I fear, tend to give a false, because one-sided,
> impression of the Rabbinic religion, and more certainly, of
> Rabbinic life. For all these legal discussions, all this 'study of the
> Law', all these elaborations and minutiae, were to the Rabbis the
> breath of their nostrils, their greatest joy and the finest portion
> of their lives. And yet to most of us, it has almost all become
> distant and obsolete: to most of us the larger part of it seems a
> waste of mental energy and of time. If a very big percentage of
> the *Halakhic* portion of the Rabbinic literature were destroyed,
> archaeology, comparative jurisprudence, and so on, would be the
> poorer, but our modern religious life would hardly be affected. . . .

Discussing Rabbinic views on Prayer, Montefiore remarks:[26]

> In spite of dull discussions and distinctions as to when you have
> fulfilled, or not fulfilled, your legal obligations concerning Prayer
> (both public and private), as to the amount of attention you need
> legally give to this prayer or to that, and so on, many noble
> reflections about prayer can be found, and much definite devel-
> opment recorded.

Montefiore's collaborator, Herbert Loewe (*A Rabbinic
Anthology* is a unique example of fruitful discussion on
Rabbinic teaching between a Liberal and an Orthodox Jew)
defends the Rabbis against the charge of irrelevance on the
grounds that *Halakhah* possesses ethical elements and these
are of permanent value.[27] Although Loewe admits the charge
of dullness he argues that dullness is the price we have to
pay for precise definitions of duty.

> By-laws are not a burden: they are essential. Yet dull they
> certainly are. No one would take as his light reading a

[23] Cf. M. Guttmann's fascinating article: *She' eloth 'Akademioth
Ba-Talmud* in *Debhir*, Vol. I, Berlin, 1923, p. 38f.
[24] Lond. 1938.
[25] p. xvi-xvii.
[26] p. xxxvi.
[27] *A Rabbinic Anthology* p. xcv.

Memorandum on Public Health, or a report on the administration of Local Option. One cannot make an entertaining anthology out of Blue Books or Local Government By-Laws.

But an alumnus of a Yeshiba would find no difficulty in refuting the charge of dullness, and could cite the exceedingly subtle novellae of Rabbi Hayyim Soloveitchick, for instance, or the *Ketzoth Ha-Hoshen* of Arye Laib Cohen, or the *Sha'are Yosher* of Rabbi Simeon Skopf, or similar standard *Halakhic* works used as textbooks in the great Yeshiboth. They may well be based on a faulty or inadequate view of the history of *Halakhah* (this point we shall shortly examine) but, most emphatically, they are anything but dull. The reading of Blue Books is dull. The making of them is quite another matter. The *Halakhic* activities of the Rabbis are to be compared with creative law-making, not with the reading of bare recorded decisions.

Despite the priority given to *Halakhic* studies, the *Torah* was a far more embracing concept. There was the whole range of the Aggada with its own specialists, the 'Rabbis of the Aggada'.[28] In the Middle Ages both philosophers, like Maimonides, and Kabbalists shifted the emphasis on to their own disciplines.[29] Jewish scholars in the past produced numerous works of profundity in *Halakhah*, but Saadiah's *Beliefs*

[28] See Weiss, *Dor*, Vol. III, Chapter 11, pp. 119-144.
[29] Cf. Maimonides' rejection of the literal interpretation of the Rabbinic saying that the Holy One, blessed be He, has no place in his world apart from the four cubits of the *Halakhah* (Introd. to *Mishnah* Comment.) and his exposition of the Rabbinic distinction between the 'great things' and the 'small things' as subjects of study to yield the thought that the former embraces metaphysics and knowledge of the physical world, the latter, *Halakhic* debate (see *Yad, Hil. Yesode Ha-Torah*, Chapter IV, 13). Cf. Isaac Husik: *A History of Mediaeval Jewish Philosophy*, Philadelphia, 1940, p. 242f. The Kabbalists, on the other hand, instead of giving priority to their subject over *Halakhah*, invested the *Halakhah* itself with esoteric meaning, see Gershom G. Scholem: *Major Trends in Jewish Mysticism*, 3rd ed. Lond., Thames and Hudson, 1955, p. 28f.

and Opinions, Bahya's *Duties of the Heart,* Maimonides' *Guide for the Perplexed,* Judah Halevi's *Kuzari,* the *Zohar* and the wealth of mystical literature, Biblical expositions, moralistic works and religious poetry point to Aggadic-inspired genius. By its most representative teachers the *Torah* was sufficiently comprehensive to justify the panegyric: 'The measure thereof is longer than the earth, And broader than the sea.'[30]

The modern Jew attempting to make the ideal of *Torah* study his own finds it more difficult than did his ancestors. The pressing problem for the modern Jew is that he cannot be as sure where the *Torah* is to be found as were the *Torah* students of the pre-critical age. He knows too much about development and evolution in Jewish beliefs and practices, he has too strong an historical sense, he has too great an awareness of the external influences always at work in shaping the pattern of Jewish life throughout the ages, to assert confidently that a passage he happens to study in the classics of Judaism is the authentic word of God. He has been compelled to re-examine the whole question of what is meant by divine inspiration. The modern believer, though he subscribes to the ancient doctrine of '*Torah* from Heaven' (*Torah min ha-shamayyim*), recognises the need for a good deal of sustained thinking on what is meant by *Torah,* by *Heaven,* and by *from!* He will tend to read his Bible with critical aids, his Talmud with the works of historical investigators to assist him, his *Kabbalah* with the recognition of its Gnostic and Neo-Platonic elements and of the universality of mysticism in the life of religion. As a believer he will not seek to eliminate the divine from human history in general or from the records of his own people's encounter with the Absolute, but he is prepared to accept that there is a human element in Revelation, that God has revealed Himself not alone *to* men but *through* men. He can appreciate the tremendous ideal of attempting to grasp the word of God but in trying

[30] Job, xi, 9.

23

to win this ideal for himself he is constantly haunted by the fear of the inauthentic. In his studies of the *Torah* there is much that is tentative, much that is speculative; convinced though he is of the great truths on which his faith is based there are areas where his intellectual honesty compels him to adopt an agnostic attitude. His quest for certainty in these areas is rarely satisfied. He says with the prophet:

> And they shall wander from sea to sea, And from the north even to the east; They shall run to and fro to seek the word of the Lord, and shall not find it.[31]

It is reported that the Gaon of Vilna once said that if he were offered infallible instruction in the *Torah* by an angel from heaven he would refuse the offer for he wanted to arrive at the truths of *Torah* through his own efforts. Solomon Schechter, in an essay on the Gaon,[32] compares this to Lessing's saying that if Truth and the Search for Truth were offered to him he would choose the Search for Truth rather than Truth. In fact, there is an important distinction, overlooked by Schechter, between the outlook of the Gaon and what appears to be that of Lessing. The Gaon's quest was not so much a search for a truth still to be realised as an attempt to understand a truth already revealed in its fullness. The Gaon would not have said that he preferred to discover the truths of religion without revelation; that he would have found more satisfaction in allowing his reason to work out a philosophy of life instead of being the recipient of a faith which maps out the life of man in all its details. He was simply saying in his own way what the Rabbis had said long before, that it was man's duty to 'labour in the *Torah*'.[33] If we use Bahya's well-known illustration of a letter from a king to his loyal subjects containing the king's requests, the Gaon would prefer the *difficult* letter to one easy to read but he

---

[31] Amos, viii, 12.
[32] *Studies in Judaism*, First Series, Philadelphia, 1896, p. 75f.
[33] *Siphra* to Lev. xxvi, 3, ed. Weiss, 110b.

would not wish to dispense with the letter itself. Lessing would prefer the subject to arrive at an understanding of the king's desires without the aid of a letter.

In Lessing's approach the only thing that is *given* is the desirability of searching for the truth. For the Gaon many more things are *given* – the existence of God, the revelation of His will in the *Torah*, the possibility and the desirability of understanding the *Torah*, in addition to the value of the quest as the supreme value. The position of the modern, religious Jew is mid-way between that of the Gaon and Lessing. For him, too, some things are *given*; there is no question of a blind search without any guarantee of success. But his search embraces a far wider field than it did for the Gaon. The *given* things are the existence of God and the belief that the *Torah* contains the revelation of His will, but the problem is complicated in that he recognises a human as well as divine element in the *Torah*. His quest is more than an attempt to *understand* the will of God. It is an attempt to *discover* the will of God.

The serpent, in the book of Genesis, asks Eve: 'Did God really say. . . ?'[34] This is the burning question which torments the modern, religious Jew. And yet he can state with conviction his belief that with regard to many of the teachings of the *Torah* the answer is, Yes. He *knows* that God did say: 'Love they neighbour as thyself',[35] 'God created man in His image',[36] 'Be holy',[37] 'Thou shalt not pervert the justice due to a stranger',[38] 'Honour thy father and thy mother',[39] 'Remember the Sabbath day to keep it holy',[40] in these and many other commands he hears unmistakably the voice of

[34] Gen. iii, 1.
[35] Lev. xix, 18.
[36] Gen. i, 27.
[37] Lev. xix, 2.
[38] Deut. xxiv, 17
[39] Ex. xx, 12.
[40] Ex. xx, 8.

God. He knows, too, that there are many things recorded in the *Torah* which God did not say, which are part of the human element in Israel's encounter with the divine. Most significant for his predicament, he feels uncertain whether some teachings are part of the divine will or whether they belong to the human element in the *Torah*. (It can be demonstrated that our ancestors were not unaware of the human element in the *Torah*[41] but for the modern Jew the problem is particularly acute because critical investigation into the sources of Judaism during the past hundred and fifty years have made most of us appreciate the extent of this element.) Is he then to limit the religious duty of *Torah* study to those matters on which there is certainty? By no means, for he recognises the capacity for distinguishing between the eternal and the ephemeral to be itself the result of *Torah* teaching. It is the *Torah* (Jewish traditional teaching about the faith) which has taught him, both directly and by moulding the Jewish character, to regard the verses quoted above as the voice of the living God and the verses concerning the extermination of the Canaanites, for one example, to be inapplicable. And this power to discern and its cultivation are themselves part of the *Torah*. The search for *Torah* is *Torah!*

In the *Torah* study of the religious Jew today the idea of a search is prominent. There is bound to be a tentativeness about many of the conclusions he reaches. For religious Jews have hardly begun to evolve a philosophy of Judaism based on sound historical investigations, a philosophy that avoids the poverties of historicism and captures the deep insights of traditional faith in a God who makes demands of His worshippers, without turning a blind eye to all that modern scholarship has achieved. Urgently required is a Jewish approach to what is now called 'Biblical Theology'. Many Christian scholars and theologians have tried to understand the implications of modern critical scholarship for their own

[41] See: L. Jacobs: *We Have Reason to Believe*, Lond., Vallentine, Mitchell, 1957, pp. 77-82.

faith. Needless to say their work, while useful in indicating the approach required, cannot profit the Jew. An essay like the chapter on 'Old Testament Theology' by Professor N. W. Porteous in *The Old Testament and Modern Study*,[42] for instance, which discusses with great learning the value of the Old Testament for Christian believers can contain little to which a devout Jew will subscribe. But Jews have much to learn from such essays of the need for assimilating the new Biblical knowledge and the 'assured results' of modern scholarship[43] in order to build a Jewish theology in which Biblical teaching is seen in the light of its application to Jewish life by the Rabbis and teachers, saints and scholars, philosophers and mystics, in every age, not forgetting the contribution of millions of Jews whose 'custom is *Torah*'.[44]

The thought that the search for *Torah* is itself *Torah* is not really so novel. It is surely implied in the whole process of

[42] Ed. H. H. Rowley, O.U.P., 1951, p. 311f.

[43] It is fashionable in some circles to deny that any results of Biblical Criticism are 'assured'. But while recognising the tentative nature of many critical views there can be no going back to a pre-critical age. Dr. Hertz, for instance, remarks that a Liberal-Jewish Critic had so absolute a faith in the Critical division of the Pentateuch according to the well-known symbols J.E.P. D.R. etc., that he permitted himself to declare: 'If one is to doubt the truth of the Critical analysis, one might just as well doubt the truth of Newton's law of gravitation!' To which Dr. Hertz retorts: 'In a statement of this nature, one sees mirrored the dogmatism of the entire school of Bible Criticism. Little did they dream of the Einsteins that were to arise, who, in the field of Physics, would restate the law of gravitation according to new categories of thought; and, in the field of Bible study, shatter the foundations of the Wellhausen hypothesis, and definitely declare its assumptions to be both unscientific and obsolete' (*The Pentateuch and Haftorahs*, Lond., Soncino, 1938, p. 399). But if the Wellhausen hypothesis is to be considered 'unscientific' surely it would be the more 'unscientific' simply to revert to the pre-critical position as if no real problems had been raised. Einstein went further than Newton, his physics are not pre-Newtonian.

[44] See *Sopherim* xiv, 18, Ber 45a.

early Rabbinic investigation known as *Midrash* (from a root meaning 'to search', 'to inquire'). The ancient teachers of Judaism carefully examined the words of the *Torah* in order to draw out their implications for the practical life of their people. The thought is implied, too, in the many discussions in the Rabbinic literature on *how* the *Torah* is to be studied, the character of the student, the subjects of study, the methods of studying, the training of students, the way of teaching and the rank and privileges of scholars. All these were looked upon as part of the *Torah;* the *Shulkhan 'Arukh* (the standard Code of Jewish law), like earlier Codes, contains a whole section on 'The Laws of *Torah* Study' which is part of the *Torah* and is, in itself, *Torah.* Judah Löwe of Prague (1525-1609) taught centuries ago: Each morning the devout Jew recites the benediction: 'Blessed art Thou . . . who commanded us to occupy ourselves with the words of *Torah.*'[45] This teacher pointed out that the form of the benediction is not 'who commanded us to study the *Torah*' for the student of *Torah* knows only too well that there are to be found frequently contradictory opinions in *Torah* literature, Rabbi *A* affirming one thing, Rabbi *B* another. The student cannot know beforehand that the opinions he wishes to understand and master belong to the true *Torah,* for he is obliged to examine the view of both Rabbi *A* and *B* and, where these are contradictory, only one can be right. But it is no part of his duty to have this knowledge. For purposes of practice, of course, some decision must be arrived at but the consideration of all the views is an essential part of the *Torah* debate. The religious duty is 'to occupy ourselves with words of *Torah*', to examine the conflicting opinions and try to arrive at the truth. Even if the student's success in arriving at the truth is limited, the attempt itself is the fulfilment of the religious duty of *Torah* study.[46]

In a bitter attack on the 'Science of Judaism', the move-

[45] *Singer's Prayer Book*, p. 4, following Ber. 11b.
[46] *Tiphereth Yisrael*, Lond., 1955, Introd., p. 2.

ment which originated in the last century in Germany and which had as its aim the objective study of Jewish thought and Jewish history, S. R. Hirsch, the famous Orthodox leader wrote:

> In fact, this learning does not want the practising Jew. For how many practising Jews actually contribute to it? How many of those who write about Selichoth, Yozeroth and Piyutim actually go to Selichoth; how many of them do not in fact banish Yozeroth and Piyutim from the liturgy? How many of those who write biographies and histories of Rabbi Jochanan ben Zakkai, of Rabbi Eliezer ben Hyrkanos, of Rabban Gamaliel, of Rabbi Akiba, of Rabbi Joshua ben Chananya etc., does the practising Jew still see following the traditions which these teachers have transmitted to us, washing their hands for instance before eating bread? . . . How many Jewish scientists does the practising Jew see treading the paths of the law alongside of himself, what inducement has he to see their science as the guide which shall help him and his children to walk before God? What has he to do with their science? Their science does not want him at all, at the utmost it will disturb him in his loyal adherence to the law, it will embitter the joy which he finds in his loyalty. With their motto of 'separation of science from faith and life' they have from the outset given up all hope of influencing actual life with their science. They have handed over the inner and outer life of the Jew to cloud and night, but in so doing they have doomed their science to remain a mere idle display of fireworks. Jewish learning ought to be the fertile soil of Jewish life, and so long as it was such it occupied the first place in actual life; but their learning is the dust from the tombs of decomposed corpses blown about over the barren steppes of the present.[47]

This is far too sweeping an indictment but because it was taken too seriously by many of Hirsch's followers their Jewish theology became divorced from historical realities, the Jewish past romanticised and Jewish teaching described in monolithic terms which left no room for the dynamic response of

[47] *Judaism Eternal – Selected Essays from the Writings of Rabbi Samson Raphael Hirsch*, Trans. by Dayan Dr. I. Grunfeld, Vol. II, Lond., Soncino, 1956, p. 290.

Judaism to the different challenges presented in different ages.

The pioneers in the field of 'Jewish Science' were bound to adhere to the principle of the 'separation of science from faith and life' so as to acquire, so far as it is humanly possible to do this, a more or less objective account of how Jewish ideas and institutions grew. They cannot be blamed if, like all pioneers, their enthusiasms made them too indifferent to the implications of the new learning for Jewish life in the present and too detached to be concerned with those implications. This one-sidedness can now be redressed. But it would be a spiritual tragedy if this were done by rejecting the tried methods of scholarship in exchange for blind worship of the past. The time has come when objectivity need not be looked upon as the fruit of neutrality towards living religious values, when the theologian can join hands with the historian in trying to grasp the word of God to our generation speaking through the pages of the past. Once the idea is accepted that the quest for *Torah* is itself *Torah* the grand old Jewish ideal of *Torah* study for its own sake is as relevant today as in the past and one that is fully compatible with the most objective approach in which the truth is followed wherever it may lead. If only a new type of Jewish scholar is permitted to emerge, who blends both the religious devotion of the old-style *talmid hakham* with the expertise, the ability to specialise in one or more great fields of Jewish learning, and the objectivity of the modern, scientific scholar, then the study of the *Torah* will once again flourish as one of the most sublime of Jewish values.

III

THE FEAR OF HEAVEN

THE fear of Heaven (*yirath shamayim*) – the Rabbinic equivalent of the Biblical 'the fear of the Lord'[1] – is the expression used in the literature of Jewish piety to denote the feeling of awe and reverence in the presence of God resulting in the unqualified desire to do His will. The second century teacher, R. Hanina, said that all things are in the hands of Heaven with the exception of the fear of Heaven.[2] This quality is the result of man's free choice. In line with this idea is the saying that before a man is born it is determined whether he is to be rich or poor, wise or foolish, healthy or sick; but the one thing undetermined is his capacity for *yirath shamayim*, it being in his own power to decide whether he is to be a *zaddik* (righteous) or a *rasha* (wicked).[3]

It is worth noting that the terms *zaddik* and *rasha* are used generally in the Rabbinic literature to describe the capacity, or lack of it, for *yirath shamayim*. This, rather than the ethical distinction, is the one made by the Rabbis. The good life is the life inspired by *yirath shamayim*, the bad life is that in which it has no place. The significance of good ethical conduct is, of course, emphasised in numerous Rabbinic teachings but, in the view of the Rabbis, ethics and religion are not synonymous. The outlook of the Rabbis was God-oriented. The point of the usual Rabbinic classification

[1] I Kings xviii, 3, 12; Job i, 9; Ps. cxii, 1; Neh. vii, 2; Lev. xix, 14, 32 and xxv, 17, 36, 43; Mal. iii, 5 and freq.
[2] Ber. 33b, Nidd. 16b.
[3] Nidd. 16b, cf. Nidd. 30b and J.E. s.v. *Fatalism*, Vol. V, p. 351.

of religious duties into those between man and God and those between man and his fellow is that both are *religious* duties – they are both called *mitzvoth,* the word, from a root meaning 'to command', used to denote a religious obligation. Man's ethical duties are divine commands. They stem from man's awareness of God's demands on him. The following Talmudic passage speaks for itself:

> Said Raba, R. Idi explained it to me: *Say ye of the zaddik, when he is good, that they shall eat the fruit of their doings*:[4] is there a *zaddik* who is good and a *zaddik* who is not good? But he who is good to Heaven and good to man, he is a *zaddik* who is good: good to Heaven but not good to man, that is a *zaddik* who is not good. Similarly you read, *Woe unto the evil rasha; for the reward of his hands shall be given unto him;*[5] is there then a *rasha* that is evil and one that is not evil? But he that is evil to Heaven and evil to man, he is a *rasha* that is evil; he who is evil to Heaven but not evil to man he is a *rasha* that is not evil.[6]

No attempt is made here to deny that the irreligious person can lead a good life in the ethical sense. The Rabbis would have parted company with those present-day religious apologists who attempt to bolster up their faith by blaming the irreligious for the lowering of moral standards. But the Rabbis saw themselves as disciples of the prophets and their function as the application of prophetic truth. The prophets invariably make their demands of justice, righteousness and mercy in the name of God. For the prophets, too, ethics are subordinate to religion in the sense that the good life is thought of by them as a whole, every part of which is God ordained and is to be God directed.

The fear of Heaven was considered to be difficult of attainment. True, say the Rabbis, Moses said: 'And now, Israel, what doth the Lord thy God require of thee, but to fear the Lord thy God . . .'[7] implying that the fear of the

[4] Is. iii, 10.
[5] Is. iii, 11.
[6] Kidd. 40a.
[7] Deut. x, 12.

Lord is easily acquired but Moses was the man of God and that which was easy for him is all too difficult for lesser mortals. The man called upon to give away an object of great value can give it willingly if he possesses it. The man called upon to give even a trivial object will find the request hard to satisfy if he does not possess it.[8] Judaism does not teach that *yirath shamayim* can be attained without effort, there would be nothing surprising to the old masters of Judaism in the lack of *yirath shamayim* among our contemporaries for little attempt is made, generally speaking, to cultivate this virtue. That great Jewish moralist, Moses Hayyim Luzzatto (1707-1747) makes this point, in the Introduction to his *The Path of the Upright,* in words which have lost none of their relevance for us:

> We read in Scripture, The fear of the Lord, that is wisdom.[9] The fear of the Lord is thus identified with wisdom, and declared to be the only true wisdom. The term 'wisdom' presupposes the use of the intellect. The truth is that the fear of God, to be properly understood, requires profound study, especially if one wants to comprehend it with the thoroughness necessary to make it part of oneself. Whoever pursues this inquiry realises that saintliness has nothing to do with what foolish pietists consider to be essential, but rather with wisdom and true perfection.[10]

That piety is the fruit of intellectual activity as well as of the devoted will may be a novel idea for the Western mind to grasp but Eastern thinkers have never countenanced the notion that man can be in touch with ultimate reality without giving to the quest considerable effort and without the cultivation of the contemplative virtues. The study of the *Torah* is not identical with *yirath shamayim*[11] but, in the

[8] Ber. 33b.
[9] Job xxviii, 28.
[10] *Mesillat Yesharim, The Path of the Upright,* ed. Mordecai M. Kaplan, Philadelphia, 1936, p. 6.
[11] See Sabb. 31a-b: 'Rabbah b. R. Huna said: Every man who possesses learning without the fear of Heaven is like a treasurer
(*Continued at foot of p.* 34)

Jewish tradition, study is a powerful aid to its attainment. Few are the Jewish saints who did not possess great learning and vigorous intellectual power.

> If thou seek her as silver, And search for her as for hid treasures; Then shalt thou understand the fear of the Lord, And find the knowledge of God.[12]

What has been said is not meant to suggest that the man who is not gifted with brain power cannot be God-fearing. The implications of the above-mentioned Rabbinic teaching that a man is born to be wise or foolish but that *yirath shamayim* is the result of his own efforts, seems to imply that even a dunce can have *yirath shamayim*. But this hardly means that any fool can have *yirath shamayim*. It is a commonplace of Jewish teaching that God rewards man according to his efforts and that far less is expected of the less gifted person. It may well be, of course, that in the eyes of God the simple, untutored pietist, whose faith is strong, is more precious than the proud scholar who glories in his learning. But this is not to say that the higher reaches of *yirath shamayim* are possible for the simple-minded. For a long time now Judaism has taught that God is to be served with the mind as well as with the heart. If this attitude leads, at times, to intellectual snobbery and spiritual pride this is a reason for the adherents of Judaism to avoid these traits. It is no reason for surrendering an approach to the religious life which calls for the participation of the keenest minds and which desires to avoid at all costs the equation of religious fidelity with ignorance and confusing sound convictions with blind enthusiasms.

But with all their regard for the quality of *yirath shamayim* the Rabbis were not oblivious to the bizarre forms its quest

who is entrusted with the inner keys but not with the outer: how is he to enter? R. Jannai proclaimed: Woe to him who has no courtyard yet makes a gate for the courtyard.' The whole passage is of importance for the Rabbinic views on the relationship between learning and piety.

[12] Prov. ii, 4-5.

could take. The history of the sects in ancient Judea towards the close of the period of the Second Temple demonstrates abundantly that the search could result in life's denial[13] and the Rabbis refused to believe that man was obliged to choose between gaining the world and gaining his soul. Something of this appears to be behind the teaching that he who enjoys the fruit of the labour of his hands is superior to the man possessing *yirath shamayim*.[14] Of the industrious worker, this passage in the Talmud continues, it is said: 'When thou shalt eat the labour of thine hands, happy shalt thou be, and it shall be well with thee'[15] – 'happy shalt thou be', in this world, 'and it shall be well with thee', in the world to come.[16]

This teaching takes us to the heart of the problem for moderns. Is *yirath shamayim* a valid aim for the religious man of today? Sensitive religious believers would probably fail to understand how the ideal can be questioned. *Yirath shamayim* is surely one of the permanent religious values. A faith deprived of it would be a faith denuded of all its power, with no ability to influence human life on the deeper levels of experience. Religion without *yirath shamayim* is no more than a sentimental attachment to ancient forms from which the spirit has departed. If moderns choose to doubt this it is because modern man has lost his religious sense. On the other hand many religious people are acutely apprehensive of the harm done, in T. H. Huxley's words,[17]

> to the citizen by ascetic other-worldliness; to the ruler, by the hatred, malice, and uncharitableness of sectarian bigotry; to the legislator, by the spirit of exclusiveness and domination; to the philosopher, by the restraints on the freedom of learning and

[13] See Louis Finkelstein: *The Pharisees*, 2nd ed., Philadelphia, 1940, pp. 8-9 and notes.
[14] Ber. 8a.
[15] Ps. cxxviii, 2.
[16] Ber. ibid.
[17] See *Approaches to the Philosophy of Religion*, ed. Daniel J. Bronstein and Harold M. Schulweis, New York, 1954, pp. 212-213.

teaching; and to the conscientious soul by the fear of theological error.

Is it possible to preserve the balance between extreme other-worldliness and materialism, between a life of religious depth which has no breadth and a life of broad but superficial vision? Following the Rabbinic interpretation mentioned above, is it possible for the man of *yirath shamayim* to have 'happiness in this world' (not in the sense of an insipid pursuit of pleasure but in the enrichment of human existence by the use of all the opportunities the modern world provides for the adventurous and the creative) with 'good in the next'?

There is no simple solution to this problem. Ever since the Emancipation there has been present in the soul of the Jew the tension between the call of the outside world and the values of his own tradition so zealously fostered in the Ghetto. But some indication of a fruitful line of approach may be found in the distinction – rooted in many of the old Jewish teachings – between two kinds of *yirath shamayim*. Many Jewish thinkers in the past have referred to higher and lower forms of this quality, the lower form being the fear of punishment which awaits the sinner, the higher form, fear in the presence of God's majesty. The fear of punishment is not really fear of God but fear of what He might do. It is a kind of self-interest in which wrong-doing is eschewed from the same motives for which insurance premiums are kept up to date. It is coldly calculating and in its worst form conceives of God as a tyrant ready to pounce on those guilty of the slightest infringement of His laws. The higher *yirath shamayim* corresponds to the sense of awe and trembling the religious man experiences when confronted by God. It is akin to the feeling described by Otto (whose views we shall shortly examine) as the 'numinous'. The *Zohar* expresses this distinction as follows:

There are three types of fear: two have no proper root, while the third is the real fear. There is the man who fears the Holy

One, blessed be He, in order that his children may live and not die, or lest he be punished in his body or his possessions; and so he is in constant fear. Evidently this is not the genuine fear of God. Another man fears the Holy One, blessed be He, because he is afraid of punishment in the other world and the tortures of Gehinnom. This is a second type which is not genuine fear. The genuine type is that which makes a man fear his Master because He is the mighty ruler, the rock and foundation of all worlds before whom all existing things are as nought.[18]

This is no isolated doctrine. The distinction between the two kinds of *yirath shamayim* is made by many of the Jewish guides to spirituality for example, Joseph Albo, the fifteenth century theologian, in his *Sepher Ha-'Ikkarim (Book of Principles of the Faith)*.[19] In the course of this author's analysis of *yirath shamayim* fear is defined as the receding of the soul and the gathering of all her powers into herself, when she imagines some fear-inspiring thing. The latter may be of two kinds. The soul may imagine a harmful thing, which she fears by reason of the injury that may come from it. Or the soul may imagine something very great, exalted, elevated and high, which she fears when she considers her own poverty and lowliness in comparison with that great thing, though she has no fear of any harm coming to her from the thing. The higher fear is the result of contemplation of the sublimity and dignity of God. The God-fearing man is ashamed to transgress His commandments just as a person is ashamed to do an unbecoming thing in the presence of an honourable prince, a respected and wise old man, who has a reputation for learning, character and dignity. Dealing with the question of why so many passages in Scripture contain the appeal to fear in the lower sense, Albo suggests that although the higher fear comes naturally to man's reason, the bodily instincts provide a hindrance to its realisation. The many references in Scripture to the lower fear have as their

[18] *Zohar* I, 11b.
[19] Trans. by Isaac Husik, Philadelphia 1946.

aim the counteracting of the bodily pull away from the higher fear so that the reason is left free to exercise its natural fascination for its Source.[20]

In a much later work, which has enjoyed the greatest popularity among the devout for two centuries, the *Mesillat Yesharim* (*The Path of the Upright*) of Moses Hayyim Luzzatto (1707-1747) referred to above, a similar analysis is found.[21] Luzzatto's famous work is an attempt to describe in detail the various rungs on the ladder of saintliness as stated by the second century teacher, R. Phinehas ben Yair. These are: watchfulness, zeal, cleanness, abstinence, purity, saintliness, humility, fear of sin, and holiness. These virtues are recorded in an ascending order of merit so that the fear of sin (which belongs to the fear of God) occupies the second highest rung. Luzzatto observes that this must refer to the higher fear for the lower type of fear is easily acquired. The lower type of fear (fear of punishment) means to fear transgressing a divine command because of the punishment, physical or spiritual, which is sure to follow. This is easy to acquire for it is natural for man to love himself and to be apprehensive about the salvation of his soul. But, continues Luzzatto, this type of fear is only for the ignorant and is unworthy of men of learning and understanding. Luzzatto evidently differs from Albo, though this is not stated explicitly, in his attitude to the appeal of Scripture to the lower fear. According to Albo this is necessary in order to check the pull of the bodily instincts and is consequently of value to all men. In Luzzatto's view it is only the 'ignorant', who lack appreciation for the higher fear, to whom this appeal is made. The solution of the modern Jew, for whom Scripture itself is the record of the divine-human encounter and contains human as well as divine elements, is that the references to 'higher' and 'lower' types of fear in Scripture show that among the Biblical writers themselves there exists a 'higher' and

[20] Vol. III, 32, p. 298f.
[21] Ed. Kaplan, Chapter XXIV, p. 211f.

'lower' approach. Obviously for thinkers of the pre-critical age like Albo and Luzzatto this solution was untenable. The whole Scripture was, for them, the direct voice of God with no possibility of contradiction in any of its parts.[22] But this is no more than a difference, albeit a significant one, in approach. For them, as for us, the highest form of *yirath shamayim* is the fear of God not the fear of what God may do. According to Luzzatto, the higher type of fear consists in refraining from sin out of regard for the glory of God. This fear is difficult of attainment for it involves comprehension of the exalted nature of God and the worthlessness of the human being. This is the fruit of deep thought and contemplation. Luzzatto distinguishes further between the concept 'fear of sin' and the concept 'fear of God' of which the former is a part. Awe in God's presence may be experienced when man is engaged in prayer or when he performs his religious duties but the fear of sin may be experienced at all times. Fear of sin means that man is constantly apprehensive of hidden snares into which he may fall. Thus, in Luzzatto's view there is a higher and lower fear of sin and a higher and lower fear of God. In their lower form the fear of sin and the fear of God are really the same thing, man being afraid to do wrong because of his fear of the consequences of wrong-doing. But on the higher level there is a distinction between the fear of sin and the fear of God. The higher fear of God is an attitude of mind and soul in which man is filled with a sense of awe at the contemplation of God's tremendous majesty. This exalted state is not possible for humans at all times. But once man has had experiences of this nature his heightened awareness of God's majesty will result in the constant state of apprehension that is designated fear of sin. Following Albo and the mediaeval thinkers generally, Luzzatto, too, remarks on the bodily instincts as hindering the attainment of this lofty degree. Man is a creature of flesh and blood. By his nature he is removed from the realm of the spiritual. Only

[22] See Louis Jacobs: *We Have Reason to Believe*, pp. 58-70.

Moses who clung devotedly to God found the fear of God easy of attainment. For lesser mortals the way to this fear is to consider that the Divine Presence is everywhere in the universe and that God's Providence extends over all things great and small. The clear realisation of God's omnipresence comes only with continual reflection and profound meditation. The matter is so remote from our comprehension that the intellect can only grasp it after severe effort and unless it is zealously cultivated it will tend to grow faint. Hence the reference in Deuteronomy 'that he may *learn* to fear'.[23] The person desirous of attaining to the higher fear of God should ponder on God's omnipresence when he sits, walks, lies down, and rises up until the truth becomes deeply rooted in his soul.

From the foregoing it will be seen that there is every support in traditional Judaism for emphasising the concept of *yirath shamayim* in the sense of religious awe rather than as a baser appeal to the emotions of fear. The evils of a terror-ridden religious faith which were noted at the beginning of this inquiry and which have certainly contributed to the widespread rejection of *yirath shamayim* are the results of interpreting the concept almost exclusively in terms of what the Zohar, Albo and Luzzatto call the 'lower fear'. It may well be that many moderns dwell all too lightly on God's judgment; the tendency nowadays is too much in favour of an easy-going attitude in which God is thought of as an indulgent Father benignly overlooking the most flagrant breaches of His laws. Modern man could benefit from the implications of many of the 'lower fear' type of passages in Scripture and in Jewish teaching generally, at least so far as the *consequences* of sin are concerned.[24] To refuse to recognise that the brutal, lustful, self-seeker harms both himself and others and that his deeds contain the germs of destruction is to live in a fool's

[23] Deut. xvii, 19.
[24] For a careful statement of this point of view see Morris Joseph: *Judaism as Creed and Life*, Lond., 1903, Chapter VII, pp. 112-137.

40

paradise. There is truth in the old Spanish proverb: 'God says, Take what you want and pay for it!' But if many moderns are too sentimental about the harsh realities of existence many of those who have spoken in the name of religion have been guilty of the dogmatism which seeks to explain man's sufferings solely in terms of his guilt. This is why it is suggested that the more fruitful approach for moderns is to stress the higher form of *yirath shamayim* and this can be done with no radical departure from traditional Jewish teaching for it is in that teaching that the distinction between the higher and lower forms is drawn.

Reference has been made to Otto. It is to the credit of this distinguished religious thinker that he has made moderns aware of 'The Idea of the Holy'[25] – to quote the title of his famous book – in terms of the 'supra-rational', that is, on its own terms not those drawn from other human experiences. In man's experience of the Holy there is a blending of fear and fascination: fear, or better, awe, in the presence of the mysterious and the unfathomable and the fascination which religious men of every age and clime have found in the adoration they freely offer to the object of their worship. Otto has called this the 'numinous' from the Latin 'numen' meaning 'spirit'. The Hebrew Bible, Otto observes, is particularly rich in the descriptions of the numinous, as is the Jewish liturgy, especially the liturgy for the 'Days of Awe' which includes among other 'numinous' prayers the supplication:

> Now therefore O Lord our God, impose Thine awe upon all Thy works and Thy dread over all Thou hast created, that all Thy works may fear Thee and all creatures prostrate themselves before Thee, that they may all form one band to do Thy will with a perfect heart. . . .[26]

Otto's 'numinous' corresponds to the 'higher *yirath shamayim*'

[25] Rudolph Otto: *The Idea of the Holy*, trans. by J. W. Harvey, 2nd ed., O.U.P., 1950.
[26] *The Festival Prayer Book*, ed. Routledge, New Year, p. 15 and frequently in the liturgy of this festival and of *Yom Kippur*.

of which the above-mentioned thinkers speak. But in addition
to tremendous mystery and fascination there is another element in the numinous as described in the Hebrew Bible. In
the book of Isaiah in particular – this prophet speaks of God
as 'the Holy One of Israel' – but in other books, too, there
is an intimate interpenetration of the numinous with the
rational and moral. In all true religious experience there is
the feeling of awe, of utter dependence, of creatureliness, of
the unworthiness of the human self when confronted by God.
This feeling is never divorced, in the Hebraic tradition,
from the moral sense and the ethical demand but it is distinct
from them. We have seen how, in the view of the Rabbis, it
is quite conceivable that a thoroughly good man, in the ethical
sense, should be utterly deficient in these feelings. Though,
for both the Rabbis and their teachers, the prophets, the
attempt to divorce religion from sound ethical conduct is
an abomination.

Otto, in discussing the numinous, produces much evidence
of its apprehension in the pages of the Hebrew Bible. For
Jews it is significant that similar passages are to be found in
the vast Rabbinic literature. The Rabbis see evidence of the
power of God in the more alarming aspects of nature, in
storms, earthquakes, thunder and lightning. The *Mishnah*
rules:

> If he saw shooting stars, earthquakes, lightnings, thunders and
> storms he should say: 'Blessed is He whose power and might
> fill the world.' If he saw mountains, hills, seas, rivers and deserts
> he should say: 'Blessed is the author of creation.'[27]

It is relevant in this connection to refer to Otto's penetrating
remarks on the numinous in the book of Job.[28] When God
appears to answer Job it is not something that can be exhaust-
ively rendered in rational concepts that is shown to Job but
the sheer absolute wondrousness in nature.

[27] Ber. IX, 2.
[28] *The Idea of the Holy*, p. 78f.

All the glorious examples from nature speak very plainly in this sense. The eagle, that 'dwelleth and abideth on the rock, upon the crag of the rock, and the strong place,' whose 'eyes behold afar off' her prey, and whose 'young ones also suck up blood, and where the slain are, there is she' – this eagle is in truth no evidence for the *teleological* wisdom that 'prepares all cunningly and well,' but is rather the creature of *strangeness* and *marvel,* in whom the wondrousness of its creator becomes apparent. And the same is true of the ostrich (xxxix, 13-18) with its *inexplicable* instincts. The ostrich is indeed, as here depicted, and 'rationally' considered a crucial difficulty rather than an evidence of wisdom, and it affords singularly little help if we are seeking *purpose* in nature: 'which leaveth her eggs in the earth, and warmeth them in the dust, and forgetteth that the foot may crush them or that the wild beast may break them. She is hardened against her young ones as though they were not hers: her labour is in vain without fear; because God has *deprived her of wisdom,* neither hath he imparted to her *understanding.'*

Otto's views have been criticised on the grounds of their 'irrationality'. The charge is hardly justified if it means that for Otto God's actions are capricious and unreasoning. Otto's point is that God is the Mind behind all creation and that there is evidence of His Mind in creation. But this must not be understood as meaning that all God's deeds can be interpreted solely in terms of human reasoning. God is what the Jewish mystics call 'higher than intelligence' – *lema'alah min ha-sekhel.* The power of the divine Mind is to be seen not alone in those of its manifestations which humans can readily apprehend but in the sheer wondrousness of nature, in those matters which cause men to marvel though they cannot understand. The Rabbis, too, speak of a special benediction to be recited on observing *strange* creatures: 'If one sees a negro, a very red or very white person, a hunchback, a dwarf or a dropsical person, he says: "Blessed is He who makes strange creatures." '[29] Similarly, 'Our Rabbis taught: On seeing an elephant, an ape, or a long-tailed ape, one says: "Blessed is

[29] Ber. 58b.

He who has such in His world."[30] The whole of Otto's book is, in fact, a reminder that 'there are *more* things in heaven and earth than are dreamt of in your philosophy'. It is hard to see why this should be understood as an attack on philosophy. Long ago the prophet said: 'For my thoughts are not your thoughts, neither are your ways my ways, saith the Lord. For as the heavens are higher than the earth so are my ways *higher* than your ways, and my thoughts than your thoughts.'[31] This is hardly a denial of the right of humans to reason but a demand, substantiated by reason, that there are realms where reason cannot penetrate.

Here the reader might ask, what is the relevance of the numinous and the higher *yirath shamayim* to the situation of modern man; are not these ideas too remote from the world of the theatre and cinema, jet propulsion and television, the popular newspaper and the coffee bar, the air liner and big business? The writer and most of the readers of this book live in a busy city; it would be sheer pretence to imagine that the contemplative virtues play any significant part in their lives. If Albo and Luzzatto, the one a deep thinker in the ages of faith, the other a visionary and mystic, both admit that the higher *yirath shamayim* is difficult of attainment, what is the Jew of today in Israel, London, New York or Paris to say? And yet if its loftiest flights are beyond the capacity of modern man the idea of the higher *yirath shamayim* is not necessarily so remote. For there are few men who cannot recognise this feeling when it is described, few who have not been profoundly stirred at one time or another by great literature, lofty music, the architecture of a house of worship, the wonders of nature,[32] or, most important of all,

[30] Ber. ibid.

[31] Is. lv, 8-9.

[32] The saying of R. Jacob (2nd cent.): 'If a man was walking by the way and studying and he ceased his study and said: "How fine is this tree!" or "How fine is this ploughed field!" Scripture reckons it to him as though he was guilty against his own soul'

(*Continued at foot of p. 45*)

the deep sense of conviction which comes from commitment to religious faith. Every religious person who really has faith has arrived at this faith as the result of experiences (differing of course, in both quality and kind from man to man) from which his sense of conviction stems. Granted that the higher *yirath shamayim* is remote from those who cannot enjoy the opportunities for contemplation envisaged by Albo and Luzzatto (and nowadays these are in the majority, even among the devout) the feeling is present in some degree in all religious people. It is not possible for man always to live on the heights. Man, teach the Jewish mystics, should acquire enough spiritual strength during the days of 'greatness of soul' (the days when his faith 'makes sense', when it is all very real to him, when his life is filled, through his belief, with a buoyant joy) to sustain him in the daily round when there is 'littleness of soul'. During these latter days *yirath shamayim* expresses itself in obedience to the will of God. In the popular Jewish idiom to say of a man that he possesses *yirath shamayim* is akin to saying that he is an observant Jew ready to do the will of God. We have examined in the previous chapter the special difficulty for moderns in recognising this will. But there is bound to be an area in which each religious Jew can say with conviction: 'I know that this is what God would have me do.' It is in this area that *yirath shamayim* operates. For it is no easy matter to do the will

('*Aboth* III, 8), has been taken to mean rejection of the idea that God can be found through the contemplation of nature. This is entirely unwarranted. R. Jacob may have been simply expressing his disapproval of the student who allows himself to be distracted *while studying*, much as a nature-loving professor would nevertheless object to his class gazing at the trees in the quad during his lecture. But even if R. Jacob's saying is interpreted as a protest against Hellenistic ideas of nature-worship this means no more than a castigation of those who would seek to *substitute* nature for the *Torah* as the supreme means of recognising the Creator. It is inconceivable that R. Jacob was unaware of the sentiments expressed in Psalms viii, 4 and xix, 2 and Isaiah xl, 26.

of God. We may be convinced beyond a shadow of doubt that a certain course of action is right and yet find it hard to comply with the right. Abraham Lincoln once said that it was not the passages in the Bible he did not understand which bothered him but the passages he did understand! To do the right thing, to live the good life, to follow the path of duty, needs powerful resources of soul. The man who has these resources and can draw on them in his daily life is a man possessed of *yirath shamayim*. In the daily prayer book of the Jew the picturesque account of the angels' song includes the words: 'All of them are beloved, pure and mighty; and all of them *in dread and awe do the will of their Master*.'[33]

The obedience of which we are thinking is not robot-like obedience. It is not incompatible with the habit of keeping an open mind on many of life's problems. It certainly does not involve the annihilation of the reason in favour of every teacher or teaching claiming to speak with authority on matters of one's religion. Indeed, the need to suspend acceptance of such teachings or even positively to combat them may be the will of God. The virtue of obedience means the willingness of a man to act upon the truth he has seen.

Obedience is due to God not to humans. It is true that in traditional Judaism much is made of obedience to Rabbinic teaching 'even if they tell thee that right is left and left right'.[34] But this is because the official teachers of Judaism were thought of as having received divine sanction for their interpretations and applications of *Torah* truths.[35] But the

---

[33] *Singer's Prayer Book*, p. 38, Cf. Maimonides: Guide III, 52 where obedience is treated not alone as the *result* of the fear of God but a means to its realisation.

[34] *Siphre* to Deut. xvii, 11. See Baruch Epstein's commentary, *Torah Temimah*, to this passage for a vigorous defence of the reading: 'Even if they *appear* to tell thee that right is left and left right.'

[35] See Sabb, 23a, Maimonides, *Sepher Ha-Mitzvoth*, Negative Precepts, 312, *Sepher Ha-Hinukh*, Precept 496, and Maimonides, *Yad, Hil. Mamrim,* Chapter I f.

idea of obedience to other humans as a means of sacrifice is quite another matter. Catholic writers have spoken of obedience to a Superior in a religious order as a 'sacrifice' which man offers to God, and of which he is himself both the priest and the victim. By poverty, it is said, he immolates his exterior possessions; by chastity he immolates his body; by obedience he completes the sacrifice, and gives to God all that he holds as his own, his two most precious goods, his intellect and his will. The sacrifice is then said to be complete and unreserved, a genuine holocaust, for the entire victim is now consumed for the honour of God.[36] It can safely be said that Judaism has too much regard for the individual will and intellect to conceive of such an obedience. Nowhere in the Jewish sources is there anything like deference to a Superior as is found, for instance, in the letters[37] of Ignatius Loyola

[36] Lejeune: *Introduction à la Vie Mystique*, 1899, p. 277, quoted by William James: *The Varieties of Religious Experience*, Lond. 1905, p. 312.

[37] William James op. cit. p. 314. In recent years among some sections of Orthodox Jewry there is to be observed a tendency to venerate, in terms similar to those employed by Ignatius Loyola, the 'great ones of Israel' i.e. the outstanding *Torah* scholars. It would be difficult to find parallels in the classic sources of Judaism to the kind of exaggerated deference recorded in a recent work in which the extremist sect of the *Neture Karta* is defended, *The Transformation*, by I. Domb, Lond., 1958, p. 73-4: '*A Godoil be-Yisroel* (*sic* = "great one of Israel") in the true sense of the term must have been born to fulfil his role. "*Before I formed thee in the womb, I knew thee*" (Jeremiah ch 1). The effort of a Jew to acquire a knowledge of *Torah*, and to approach the higher degrees of personal holiness, can achieve only as much as the individual in question is *equipped* to achieve. . . . The words and decisions of the genuine *Godoil be-Yisroel*, are not only binding with regard to matters of direct *Torah* concern; they affect everything to which the assumption of an attitude is demanded. The true *Godoil* does *not* need to support his words *with proof* or argument. For he *himself* is so closely identified with *Torah* that even his thoughts constitute *Torah*, and his views unconsciously and effortlessly reflect the loftiest source of wisdom' (italics the author's).

(with the possible exception of some *Hasidic* texts which speak of the honour due to the leader, the *Zaddik*):

> In the hands of my Superior, I must be a soft wax, a thing, from which he is to require whatever pleases him, be it to write or receive letters, to speak or not to speak to such a person, and the like; and I must put all my fervour in executing zealously and exactly what I am ordered. I must consider myself as a corpse which has neither intelligence nor will; be like a mass of matter which without resistance lets itself be placed wherever it may please any one; like a stick in the hand of an old man, who uses it according to his needs and places it where it suits him. So must I be under the hands of the Order, to serve it in the ways it judges most useful.

The Rabbis, too, use the simile of a corpse in the famous statement that the *Torah* can only exist permanently in he who makes himself as one dead on its behalf,[38] but the reference here is to the assiduous study of the *Torah* which involves severe self-denial.

Another point of much significance with regard to the virtue of obedience in the Jewish tradition is that it has to be exercised chiefly on one's own behalf and not gratuitously on behalf of others. Rabbi Israel Salanter (1810-1883), the founder of the religious-ethical movement known as the *Musar* movement, was particularly zealous in stressing the wrongness of, as he put it, using another's shoulders as stepping stones to piety. Of this saint it is said that contrary to established religious practice he would use only the bare minimum of water for the ritual washing of the hands before meals because, for him, the water had to be carried laboriously from the well by the poor overworked and underpaid servant girl. Once while staying over the Sabbath at the home of a pupil he refused to sing the traditional Sabbath table hymns and he rushed through the meal in order to give the cook, who had been working hard all day, an early opportunity to retire to her well-earned rest.[39]

[38] Ber. 63b.
[39] On Israel Salanter and the *Musar* movement see especially, Dobb Katz: *Tenuath Ha-Musar*, Tel-Aviv, 1950-56, Vol. I-III.

THE FEAR OF HEAVEN

It is a common fault of the man strict with himself to be as uncompromisingly severe with others, condemning their faults as harshly as he condemns his own so that piety leads to censoriousness. It was this that the founder of the *Hasidic* movement, Israel Baal Shem Tob (the *Besht*), (1700-1760) had in mind when he said that the *zaddik,* the righteous man, is a *'schlechter'*. The saying of the *Besht* is worth quoting in full. The *Besht* spoke of the faults of virtuous men. The intellectual, he said, is a cynic and a heretic. The good-natured man is a fool; by which he no doubt referred to the man who is 'generous to a fault' or to the type of person described by, 'She goes through life doing good to others; you can tell the others by their hunted look.' And the righteous man is bad (a *schlechter*): critical of himself he cannot help uncharitably condemning others. But, went on the *Besht* to ask, if the intellectual is a cynic, the good-natured man a fool, and the righteous man a kill-joy, what is a man to do? Is it not his duty to be wise, good and righteous? He has to be all three, was the *Besht's* answer, and then the virtues of each will effectively offset the vices of the others. Righteousness will mitigate against the evils of a detached intellectualism, wisdom will prevent goodness degenerating into folly, and goodness will temper the harshness of stern, unbending righteousness. *Yirath shamayim* is a great Jewish virtue. But, perhaps more than any other, it can do harm if it is allowed to function in isolation. But it was never intended that it function in isolation. Combined with the other Jewish values it has the power of bringing firmness to the Jewish character and nourishment to the Jewish soul.

IV

THE LOVE OF GOD

SOME of the critics of Judaism have said that it is a religion based on fear. God is a severe master and He rules His subjects with a rod of iron. A strange description of the faith of the Psalmist: 'As the hart panteth after water brooks, so panteth my soul, after Thee, O God'![1] Or of the religious outlook of the book of Deuteronomy, a book brimming with tenderest expressions of God's love for Israel and Israel's love of God, and which contains the *Shema*, Israel's declaration of faith. The *Shema* begins with the words: 'Hear (*Shema*), O Israel, the Lord our God, the Lord is One'[2] to be followed by the verse: 'And thou shalt love the Lord thy God with all thy heart, and with all thy soul, and with all thy might.'[3] Or of the faith of the Rabbis who said:

> It is written: 'The righteous shall flourish like the palm tree.'[4] As the palm tree directs its heart upward, so the Israelites direct their heart to their Father in heaven. As the palm tree has its yearning, so the righteous among them have their yearning. Towards what is this yearning? Towards God, the Holy One. R. Tanhuma said: There was a palm tree which stood in *Hamethan,* and it bore no fruit, and they fertilised it, but it bore no fruit. Then a palm-planter said to them: 'It sees a palm tree of Jericho, and it yearns after it in its heart.' So they brought some of the palm tree from Jericho, and they fertilised the first palm tree,

[1] Ps. xlii, 2.
[2] Deut. vi, 4.
[3] Deut. vi, 5.
[4] Ps. xcii, 13.

and it bore fruit at once. So all the yearning and the hope of the righteous are turned towards God.[5]

Or of Maimonides, who interpreted the Rabbinic saying that three died with a divine kiss to mean that these three died in the midst of the pleasure derived from the knowledge of God and their great love for Him.[6] Or of the *Hasidim* who taught that the main thing is to encompass oneself in the love of God, the love of Israel, and the love of the *Torah*.

That Judaism enjoins the love of God can only be denied by its most prejudiced critics,[7] but the most devoted of its followers have found it far from easy to understand the correct meaning of the love of God and how to live by the ideal. It is not difficult for concrete things, tangible objects, to awaken love. Rupert Brooke's 'Great Lover' states his fondness for white plates and cups, for grainy wood, for roofs wet with rain in the lamplight, for burning leaves, all of them things to which the senses are attracted. We can understand, too, the love of an artist for his work, the thinker for his ideas, the devotee of literature for his books. But how can man come to love the Invisible King? How can man love God, still more difficult, how can he be commanded to love God? Can love ever be commanded? Is not spontaniety of love's essence so that to make it a duty is to destroy it? (There is much power in the thought that God loves man so much that He must *command* man to love Him. He wants, as it were, man's love so much that He cannot leave it to man's choice if He is to be loved. He must command just as the lover tries to compel

---

[5] Num. R. III, 1. The meaning of 'directs its heart upwards' appears to be that the palm tree, unlike other trees which curve, grows straight upwards.

[6] Guide III, 51 end.

[7] For a fully documented study of Jewish teachings on this theme see Georges Vajda: *L'amour de Dieu dans la Théologie Juive du Moyen Age*, Paris, 1957. Vajda's book deals comprehensively with much that has been written on the subject, from the close of the Talmud to the expulsion of the Jews from Spain.

his beloved to reciprocate his affections.[8] But the difficulty remains, is a commanded love not a contradiction in terms? There are, on the whole, two answers to these questions in the Jewish tradition, two different approaches to the love of God.

The first is the mystical approach in which the love of God is that yearning for nearness to the Source of all being that is characteristic, if we can judge by its recorded instances, of all mystics. This love is generally said to be, by those who are recognised masters in this field, the fruit of contemplation. As some of the Jewish mystics say, it follows on the fear of God in the higher sense in which that fear has been described in the previous chapter. The connection between the fear and love of God and the need for contemplation if these are to be attained is taught by Maimonides:

> What is the way to His love and fear? When man considers His great and wonderful deeds and creatures and observes in them His incomparable and limitless wisdom he immediately loves and praises and glorifies and has a great desire to know the great Name. As David said: 'My soul thirsteth for God, for the living God.'[9] And when man thinks on these very things he immediately steps backwards in awe and he experiences fear and dread in the knowledge that he is a puny creature of lowly darkness standing with his small and insignificant mind before the Perfect in knowledge. As David said: 'When I behold Thy heavens, the work of Thy fingers, The moon and the stars, which Thou hast established; What is man, that Thou art mindful of him?'[10] [11]

In greater detail, Bahya Ibn Pakudah (10th or 11th cent.) the famed author of *The Duties of the Heart*, similarly attaches

---

[8] Cf. Sabb. 88a: ' "And they stood under the mount" (Ex. xix, 17): This teaches that the Holy One, blessed be He, overturned the mountain upon them like an inverted cask, and said to them: "If ye accept the *Torah*, 'tis well; if not, there shall be your burial." '

[9] Ps. xlii, 3.

[10] Ps. viii, 4-5.

[11] *Yad, Hil. Yesode Ha-Torah*, II, 2.

the greatest importance to contemplation as an aid to the love of God:

> Which is the way to the love of God? I reply that this question can only be put after many conditions, from which the love of God is born, are fulfilled. But he who intends to possess that love in itself (i.e. without the conditions being fulfilled) will never reach his goal. The conditions which the believer should observe are the following: two unifications, two abasements of the heart, two reflections, and two proofs. Of the two unifications, one is for the heart to be united with God, the second to unite one's deeds to His name and to serve Him for His glory alone. Of the two abasements of the heart, one is to humble oneself before the exalted God, the second is to humble oneself before those who fear God and before His chosen ones. Of the two reflections, one is to consider the obligations man owes to God because of His constant goodness, the second to consider how God hides man's sins and waits patiently to grant him pardon. Of the two proofs, one is the evidence gained from the past, the result of reading the prophetic books and the words of the early teachers, on whom be peace, as it is said: 'I remember the days of old.'[12] The second is the evidence gained from the observance of the wonders of the blessed Creator in His creatures. . . . If he ponders on these things and in addition abstains from the pleasures and lusts of the world, if he understands the greatness of God, His power, truth and glory and is aware of his own lowliness and insignificance, if he recognises the Creator's great goodness to him and the abounding lovingkindness He has shown to him, the love of the believer for God will follow with perfect heart and true purification of soul. . . . The most powerful of the things which help man to achieve this lofty state is the great fear of God, the dread of Him, and the terror of His commands, as well as the constant thought that He looks into thy secret heart and sees thee and His care for thee and His pity for thee, and His knowledge, both hidden and revealed, in the past and the future, of thy deeds and thoughts, and His promise to thee. . . .[13]

One of the great mystics of this century was Abraham Isaac Kook, the first Chief Rabbi of Palestine (b. Latvia, 1864; d. Jerusalem, 1935). Kook was one of the most original Jewish

[12] Ps. cxliii, 5.
[13] *The Gate of Divine Service*, Chapter III, cf. Chapter IV.

thinkers in modern times, directing his ideas especially to the problem of capturing the message of eternal Judaism for our scientific and technological age. Kook is reported to have said that the atheist and unbeliever fulfil an important function in their attacks on crude belief in that they compel believers to attain a purer, more exalted conception. It would be futile to pretend that Kook's prolific writings make for easy reading. But the following quotation gives some idea of how this famous contemporary mystic understood the love of God:

> Faith chiefly involves the conception of God's greatness so that whatever the heart conceives is as nought compared with that which it is fitting to conceive, and this, in turn, is as nought compared to the Reality. All the divine names, whether in Hebrew or in other languages convey no more than a faint spark of the hidden light for which the soul longs and which it gives the name 'God'. Every definition of the divine leads to denial and all attempts at defining the divine are spiritual idolatry. Even the definition of divine intellect and will and even the divine itself and the name 'God' are definitions and lead to denial unless they are qualified by the higher knowledge that these are but the light of sparks flashing from that which is above definition. . . . It is a natural thing for all creatures to be submissive to the divine, for all particular being to be as nought before Being in general, how much more before the Source of all general Being? In this there is nothing of pain or repression but only delight and strength, majesty and inner power. . . . When the central point of the recognition of the divine is weak the divine Existence is thought of as no more than a tyrannical force from which there is no escape and before which one must be subdued. He who approaches the service of God in this empty situation, when the lower fear of God is torn from its source in the higher fear through the dark conception of the divine, arrived at as a result of the lack of intelligence and of *Torah*, gradually loses the illumination of his world. The majesty of God cannot then be revealed in the soul, only the degraded conceptions of an unbridled imagination, which portrays an obscure and false image calculated to confuse he who believes in it and to crush his spirit and remove all the divine splendour from his soul. Even if such a person proclaims all day long that this is belief in the One

God this is no more than an empty phrase of which the soul knows nothing.[14]

Rabbi Kook taught that man by nature is a mystic. A favourite poem composed by Kook speaks of his longing for 'expanses':

> Expanses, expanses,
> Expanses divine, my soul doth crave.
> Enclose me not in cages
> Of matter or mind.
> Through heavenly vastness my soul doth soar
> Unfenced by walls of heart
> Or walls of deed –
> Of ethics, logic, or mores –
> Above all these it soars and flies,
> Above the expressible and nameable,
> Above delight and beauty.[15]

Describing the thought of his father, Rabbi Kook's son, in an interview with an American Rabbi, said:

People associate love with sentimental feeling alone. But love includes much more. The act of love should bring all levels of the human being into play, his intuitions, his emotions, and his logic and mind as well.[16]

It is good for us to know the teachings of the great Jewish masters of the past on this exalted subject even if we cannot hope to approximate to their longing for God. But if we do not find it within us to make their mystical yearning our own ideal except in very restricted measure does this mean that the loving of God is beyond us? By no means. For Judaism knows of another approach to the love of God for those with no mystic pretensions. The dominant interpretation of the

[14] See *Perakim Bemahashebheth Yisrael*, ed. S. Israeli, Israel, 1952, pp. 77-78.
[15] J. B. Agus, *Banner of Jerusalem* (a biography of Kook), New York, 1946, p. 130.
[16] Rabbi H. Weiner in *Commentary*, 1954, p. 258. This article and the book quoted in the previous note are the best introductions in English to Rabbi Kook's thought.

love of God in the Rabbinic literature makes this ideal possible of realisation in more mundane, but no less heroic, fashion. The genuine mystic has achieved the higher flights of religious experience. But there is something morbid and unhealthy in an *artificial* longing, by those with no mystical powers of soul, for spiritual excitement and titillation, especially if this results in a contempt for the hard round of daily duty. The *Siphre,* one of the earliest Rabbinic works on the Bible, states the problem and its solution in terms readily comprehensible by normal men and women: 'We are told to love God,' asks the *Siphre,* 'but how can man love God?' The *Siphre* replies by referring to the verse in Deuteronomy which follows on the command to love:

> 'And these words, which I command thee this day, shall be upon thy heart; and thou shalt teach them diligently to thy children, and shall talk of them when thou sittest in thy house, and when thou walkest by the way, and when thou liest down, and when thou risest up.'[17] Take these words of the *Torah* to thy heart, interprets the *Siphre,* and in this way learn to acknowledge Him at whose word the world came into being and cleave to His paths.[18]

Men have found God in many ways, through nature and the pursuit of beauty, in the promptings of conscience, through the search for order and harmony in the universe, but the Rabbinic approach is to find God through the *Torah* and its precepts, through the study of His word and its application to life. According to the *Siphre,* the command to love God does not belong to the mystical or the ecstatic. By studying the *Torah* and carrying out its precepts, by living a life of justice, righteousness and humility, man's existence is illumined with the light of the divine. In the words of Abraham Joshua Heschel, a distinguished modern Jewish religious thinker, he perceives the infinite in doing the finite. The *Siphre* does not suggest that the *Torah* life *leads* to the

[17] Deut. vi, 6-7.
[18] *Siphre* to Deut. vi, 5.

love of God but that it *is* the love of God. If we try to analyse
the thought of the authors of the *Siphre* the result would
probably be something like this. In speaking of the love of
God the *Torah* is describing a conception very difficult for
us to grasp. But the *Torah* speaks to human beings and there
must be a sense in which this word of the *Torah* can be
appreciated and acted upon by ordinary men and women.
A lover is delighted at his opportunities for carrying out his
beloved's wishes. The commands of the *Torah* are the will
of God and consequently the command to love means that we
behave towards God as the lover behaves towards his beloved
and we carry out the precepts of the *Torah*. This approach
is less spectacular than the mystical interpretation of the love
of God but it is one less capable of perversion by self-delusion
and more possible of realisation by the majority. Judaism
has its mystics and deep religious thinkers. For these and their
followers only the higher approach to the love of God will
satisfy. Nor is this approach completely foreign in the
Rabbinic tradition. But the teaching of the *Siphre* is still the
most effective one for ordinary men and women. There is at
least some truth in Renan's famous remark that, to the
Christian, religion is his sweetheart, to the Jew, his lawful
wedded wife.

This approach, too, is impossible without cultivation. The
appreciation of great painting is not developed by a casual
stroll through an art gallery nor a taste for splendid music
by an occasional visit to the concert hall. The art or music
lover may start by merely knowing what he likes but if he
is serious he studies the techniques of the greatest practi-
tioners and perhaps tries his own hand at the subject until
his appreciation is deepened.

It will be seen that the question with which this discussion
opened – how can man be commanded to love God? – is
solved, in the Jewish tradition in two ways. In the mystical
and philosophical tradition the command is understood as a
command to contemplate and to reflect on God's majesty, for

this leads to the love of God. In the general Rabbinic tradition the command is interpreted as a command to perform certain deeds (these, unlike the emotions, can be ordered) and these deeds, in themselves, constitute the love of God. If we have understood the *Siphre* correctly the command to *love* means the command to *do* (the study of the *Torah* and the carrying out of its precepts). Here the logical positivist might object that you cannot call one thing another and say it means that other thing unless this meaning is the one given to the thing in everyday parlance. But this objection would only be valid if, in fact, there were no point of correspondence between the term 'loving God' and the term 'doing the things the *Torah* commands'. But, as we have seen, and as must be obvious, there *is* a point of correspondence, for the lover does certain things – the fulfilment of his beloved's desire – as a consequence and as a token of his love. It is not therefore nonsense to equate the love of God with the fulfilment of the *Torah*, God's word.

In line with this approach is the Rabbinic comment on the command to love God 'with all thy heart and with all thy soul and with all thy might'.[19] The *Mishnah*[20] prefers to understand these less as abstract states of mind than patterns of behaviour to be adopted in given situations:

'With all thy heart,' with both thine impulses, thy good impulse and thine evil impulse; 'and with all thy soul' – even if He take away thy soul; 'and with all thy might' – with all thy wealth – for whichever measure He measures out to thee, do thou give Him thanks exceedingly.

This *Mishnah* teaching is important. The *Mishnah* is the great Code of Jewish law and practice. Its non-legal portions are few and when they occur enjoy great authority. The editor of the *Mishnah* must have thought these non-legal passages important enough to place them in juxtaposition with accepted teachings and decisions. Consequently, a pass-

[19] Deut. vi, 5.
[20] Ber. IX, 5.

age such as this interpretation of the verse on love may be said to be official Rabbinic teaching. It is worthwhile examining this passage in greater detail in accordance with the expositions given to it in the *Gemara* and the commentaries.

The *Mishnah* attaches homiletical significance to the fact that the Hebrew word for heart in the phrase 'with all thy heart' duplicates the letter *beth – lebhabh,* instead of *lebh.* This is said to mean that man must love God with both his hearts, that is, to serve Him with both the good inclination and the evil inclination. The most probable meaning of this is that God can be served with the bodily and egoistic instincts as well as with the spiritual and altruistic ones. The idea that the *yetzer hara* (the evil inclination) has its place in human life and can be used in God's service (a doctrine with suggestive affinities to modern theories on 'sublimation') is basic to Rabbinic Judaism.[21] It is true that although some of the mediaeval Jewish thinkers, under the influence of Greek views of a dualistic nature, tended to emphasise the *evil* of the evil inclination, this tendency is really a departure from the mainstream of Rabbinic thought which on the whole recognises that the evil inclination, too, can be used in the service of the good. There is a well-known passage in which it is said that without the sex instinct and without ambition (both referred to as the 'evil inclination') a man would neither marry nor build a house in which to live and civilisation would be destroyed.[22] In an even more remarkable passage the illustration is given of a king who wounded his son in anger. The king gave the son a plaster to place on the wound saying:

> As long as this plaster is on the wound you can eat and drink whatever you desire and the wound will not fester. But if you remove the plaster from the wound and then eat and drink whatever you desire the wound will fester.

[21] See Chapters XV and XVI in S. Schechter's: *Some Aspects of Rabbinic Theology,* Lond., 1909, pp. 242-292.
[22] *Yalkut, Bereshith* 16 on Gen. i, 31.

The wound is the evil inclination which God (=the king) inflicts upon man. The *Torah* is the plaster on the wound.[23] In other words, there is no need for man to abstain from a normal life and attempt to deny himself in ascetic practices in order to defeat the evil potentialities of his nature. The *Torah* and its precepts are sufficient to control man's nature. Judah Ha-Levi (b. *c.* 1080) is a true disciple of the Rabbis in this matter. In his book *Kuzari* Judah Ha-Levi makes his Rabbinic defender say:

> The divine law imposes no asceticism on us. Rather it desires that we keep the equipoise, and grant every mental and physical faculty its due, as much as it can bear, without overburdening one faculty at the expense of another. If a person gives way to licentiousness he blunts his mental faculty; he who is inclined to violence injures some other faculty. Prolonged fasting is no act of piety for a weak person who, having succeeded in checking his desires, is not greedy. For him feasting is a burden and self-denial. Neither is diminution of wealth an act of piety, if it is gained in a lawful way, and if its acquisition does not interfere with study and good works, especially for him who has a household and children. He may spend part of it in almsgiving, which would not be displeasing to God; but to increase it is better for himself. Our law, as a whole, is divided between *fear, love* and *joy*, by each of which one can approach God. Thy contrition on a fast day does nothing to bring thee nearer to God than thy joy on the Sabbath and holy days, if it is the outcome of a devout heart. . . .[24]

'With all thy soul' is taken by the *Mishnah* to mean, 'even if He take away the soul'.[25] This is to say that there are times when a Jew is expected to give his life for his faith and suffer martyrdom rather than betray his religion. Jewish history records numerous instances of martyrdom for the faith by loyal Jews and Jewesses. Early on in the literature of Jewish piety this was taken to embrace the many acts of self-denial

[23] Kidd, 30b.
[24] *Kuzari* II, 50, ed. H. Hirschfield, Eng. trans., Lond., 1931, p. 99.
[25] The Hebrew word *nephesh* (translated as 'soul') frequently means 'life', see B.D.B., s.v.

and self-sacrifice which the good man is frequently called upon to make. One of the names for martyrdom in Jewish tradition is *mesirath nephesh*, lit. 'giving up the soul', probably based on this *Mishnah*. And the term is used not only for the supreme sacrifice but as a synonym for severe self-denial in the service of the good. A man who has struggled against great odds to build a Synagogue or a house of learning is said to have laboured with *mesirath nephesh*.

'With all thy might' is taken by the *Mishnah* to mean 'with all thy wealth'. Wealth is power[26] and this, too, must be sacrificed if God so demands. The *Shulkhan 'Arukh*, the standard Code of Jewish Law, contains detailed regulations on the extent of this sacrifice.[27] The interpretation includes, of course, the obligation to spend one's wealth liberally and generously in the cause of religion and in the giving of charity.

Finally, the *Mishnah* gives another interpretation to 'with all thy might' – 'for whichever measure He measures out to thee, do thou give Him thanks exceedingly.' The point here can be understood if we know that it is a common form of Rabbinic exegesis to use an ingenious play on words as a means of conveying important lessons. The Hebrew for 'thy might' is *meodekha*. The root meaning of this word is 'to exceed' and it resembles in sound two other Hebrew words – *middah*, 'a measure', and *modeh*, 'to give thanks'. Hence the interpretation: 'for whichever *measure* (*middah*) He measures out to thee, do thou give Him thanks (*modeh*) exceedingly (*meod*).' The idea here is that loving God with all one's might means accepting all that befalls one, whether good or evil, in the spirit of submission. As this *Mishnah* puts it: 'Man is bound to bless God for the evil even as he blesses God

---

[26] Cf. ' "And all the substance that was at their feet" (Deut. xi, 6) R. Eleazar said: This refers to a man's wealth, which puts him on his feet' (Sanh. 110a).
[27] *Yoreh De'ah* 157: 1 and 249: 1-2.

for the good.'[28] Later teachers rose to the heights of interpreting this to mean that man should bless God for the evil *in the same spirit of joy* in which he blesses God for the good! Beyond the reach of most men though it is, this interpretation has been sealed by the mode of living of not a few Jewish saints.[29]

An integral part of the love of God is the pure motive. Religious teachers are generally agreed on the significance to religion of disinterestedness. The love of God and obedience to His will, these ought to be the motives for doing good and not the desire for gain. The man who leads the good life for what he can get out of it, whether in winning the esteem and admiration of others, or, as many of the saints have said, even on the higher level in anticipation of spiritual bliss in the Hereafter, is more self-worshipper than worshipper of God. Dean Inge has finely remarked:[30]

> The main argument of Lippmann's book (*Preface to Morals*) is that 'disinterestedness' is the vital part of higher religion. Aldous Huxley has since said the same, calling it, less happily, non-attachment. When I was ordained deacon by the saintly Bishop of Lincoln . . . the only thing that the Bishop said to me was 'Be disinterested; that is what really matters.' Perhaps no wiser counsel could be given to a young man who might be suspected of being ambitious. I have always remembered it; though I have taken occasion to say, 'Don't fancy yourself disinterested when you are only uninterested, and don't fancy yourself attracted by God when you are only repelled by man!'

'I stand between the Lord and between you. . . .'[31] was penetratingly interpreted by a late *Hasidic* master, with the exegetical licence the teachers of the movement allowed

---

[28] Ber. IX, 5.
[29] See *Bertinoro* to Ber. IX, 5 and the extracts from the testament of Alexander Suesskind and the short introduction in Israel Abraham's: *Hebrew Ethical Wills*, Philadelphia, 1948, pp. 327-341.
[30] *Diary of a Dean*, Lond., Hutchinson, 1949, p. 155.
[31] Deut. v, 5.

themselves, to yield the thought that the 'I' – man's grasping ego – acts as a barrier between him and his Maker.

Antigones of Sokho, one of the earliest teachers whose views are recorded in Talmudic literature, is reported as saying:

> Be not like slaves that minister to the master for the sake of receiving a bounty, but be like slaves that minister to the master not for the sake of receiving a bounty: and let the fear of Heaven be upon you.[32]

R. Jose (early second century c.e.) taught,

> Let all thy deeds be done for the sake of Heaven,[33]

a doctrine understood by later teachers as embracing not alone religious duties but all the acts of man. In this view Jewish saintliness consists in thinking of God and directing the mind Godwards in whatever a man does, so that even the indulgence of the bodily needs should not be for self-gratification but as an act of worship.

> Whatever benefit a man derives from this world, his intention should not be for his own pleasure but to serve the Creator, blessed be His name. As it is written: 'In all thy ways acknowledge Him.'[34] The Sages say: 'Let all thy deeds be done for the sake of Heaven.' That is to say even legitimate things such as eating and drinking, walking, sitting and standing, sexual intercourse, conversation and all the needs of thy body should all be attended to in the service of thy Creator or for that which brings about His worship. For even if a man is thirsty or hungry, it is not praiseworthy if he eats and drinks for his own pleasure but he should have the intention of eating and drinking to gain strength to serve God. Similarly, even to sit in the meeting-place of the upright and to walk in the counsel of the perfect is not praiseworthy if a man does these things for his own pleasure to carry out his own needs and desires, but only for the sake of

[32] *'Aboth* I, 3. Another reading is 'But be like slaves that minister for the sake of not receiving a bounty' – '*al menath shelo,* instead of *shelo 'al menath* – implying a positive rejection of all rewards, see *Tos. Yom Tobh* ad loc.

[33] *'Aboth* II, 12

[34] Prov. iii, 6.

Heaven. So, too, with regard to sleeping, it goes without saying that a man ought not to indulge in sleep to please himself at a time when he can be occupied in the study of the *Torah* and the practice of its precepts but even when he is tired and obliged to rest it is not praiseworthy if he rests to give pleasure to his body but his intention should be to give sleep to his eyes and rest to his body for the sake of his health so that his mind should not be confused through lack of sleep when he studies the *Torah*. Similarly, with regard to the duty of sexual intercourse mentioned in the *Torah*, it is despicable if a man performs the act to fulfil his desire or to give pleasure to his body. And even if his intention is to have children who will minister to his needs and take his place it is not praiseworthy. But his intention should be to have children who will serve his Creator or his intention should be to fulfil the precept of visiting his wife in her time like a man who pays his debt. So, too, with regard to conversation, even when speaking words of wisdom it is necessary for his intention to be for the service of his Creator or for that which brings about His worship. The general principle is that a man is obliged to set his eyes and his heart on his ways and to weigh all his actions in the balance of his mind and when he sees that an action will lead to God's service let him do it. Otherwise, let him refrain from doing it. He who behaves in this way serves the Creator all the time.[35]

This extension of the principle, 'Let all thy deeds be done for the sake of Heaven', according to which man's instincts were created for no other purpose than to provide him, as it were, with the opportunity for transcending them in a spiritual athleticism, is hardly in accord with the modern religious temper which favours a less rigorous and less hostile attitude to the body and its needs. Nowadays, we would be inclined to say that God is served by the legitimate indulgence of the instincts He has created, or, at least, that the physical pleasure attendant on the act is not to be looked upon as a necessary evil to bring about the 'higher' aim for which the act was intended, but as a good in itself. Needless to say, in the wide range of Jewish religious teaching and experience both the puritanical and anti-puritanical moods

[35] *Shulkhan 'Arukh, 'Orah Hayyim*, 231, 1.

find expression. It is undoubtedly true that in the mediaeval literature the austere mood predominantly prevails, but in the earlier Rabbinic literature the less severe attitude is demonstrated in the dictum that a man will be held accountable to God for refusing to enjoy the things he is permitted to enjoy.[36]

Be this as it may, there is complete unanimity in the classical sources on the need for disinterestedness in the performance of religious duties. The few apparent contradictions, expressing a less heroic view, were inevitably smoothed away by the commentators. When a second century source, for instance, teaches that he who declares: 'This coin be for charity that my son may live' or 'that I might merit the future world' is completely righteous,[37] it seemed obvious for the famed *Mishnah* commentator, Yom Tobh Lippmann Heller (1579-1654) to remark that he is a righteous man (*zaddik*) if he thinks of reward but he is no saint[38] (*hasid*). Disinterested service is the *sine qua non* of saintliness.

> 'Let not a man say,' another Talmudic passage has it, 'I will read Scripture that I may be called a Sage; I will study that I may be called a Rabbi; I will teach to be an Elder, and sit in the seat of the elders'; but learn out of love, and honour will come in the end.[39] R. Eliezar son of R. Zadok (second century C.E.) said: 'Do good deeds for the sake of their Maker, and speak of them for their own sake. Make not of them a crown wherewith to magnify thyself, nor a spade to dig with.'[40]

The Rabbinic doctrine of 'for the sake of Heaven' (*leshem shamayim*)[41] corresponds to the ideal of disinterestedness but

[36] Yer. Kidd. IV, 12. Cf. the discussion in M. H. Luzzatto's *Mesillat Yesharim*, Chapter XIII, ed. Kaplan, Philadelphia, 1936, p. 118f.

[37] Pes. 8b.

[38] Comment. to *'Aboth* I, 3, advanced in order to solve the contradiction between this saying and that of Antigones, cf. Tos. Pes. 8b s.v. *sheyizkeh*.

[39] Ned. 62a.

[40] Ned. ibid.

[41] A distinction must be drawn between the Rabbinic idea of
(*Continued at foot of p. 66*)

is more positive in that it calls attention to the Object towards which the mind should be directed. 'Purify our hearts to serve Thee in truth' is the expression of this ideal in the language of prayer.

> "Why is it,' asked Joseph Dobh Soloveitchick the renowned Rabbi of Brest-Litovsk, 'that those who work for falsehood frequently succeed, while those who work for truth often fail? Because, those who work for falsehood do so in truth but those who work for truth do so in falsehood!'

Disinterestedness is more than the absence of hypocrisy. The *Oxford Dictionary* defines hypocrisy as the *simulation* of virtue or goodness. The hypocrite is acting a part. The aims he ostensibly avows are not his true aims. His behaviour is no more than a cloak which he dons to fool others or, where the hypocrisy is unconscious, to fool himself. As La Rochefoucauld said, 'hypocrisy is the homage paid by vice to virtue'. It follows that the disinterested man cannot be a hypocrite but it by no means follows that the man who is not a hypocrite is disinterested. A man may be entirely sincere in his motivation, he may be convinced beyond doubt that his aim is the right one but he may, nonetheless, pursue that aim for his own gain. For instance, the man who gives generously to a cause of which in his heart of hearts he disapproves, in order to win the esteem of others, is a hypocrite. The man

lishmah and that of *kavvanah*, frequently, but erroneously, identified with each other in contemporary writings on Judaism. *Lishmah* refers to the *motive* behind the performance of a religious duty, *kavvanah* to the *concentration* involved. When a person carries out a religious duty with an ulterior motive but is fully aware that what he is doing is a religious duty there is an absence of *lishmah* but no lack of *kavvanah*. Conversely, he may have the sincere desire to carry out his duty 'for the sake of Heaven' but may allow his mind to wander in the performance. Here *kavvanah* is absent but not *lishmah*. The prig who prays that men may admire him offends against the *lishmah* idea. The well-intentioned worshipper who lacks the power of concentration offends against the *kavvanah* idea.

who gives with the same self-seeking motive to a cause he holds to be worthy thinks of himself but is no hypocrite. The disinterested man gives to the good cause in order to further that cause.

Is disinterestedness desirable? Not so strange a question in spite of the significance attached to the ideal in religious thought, for it might be argued that there is no more powerful incentive to action than self-interest and the felicity of mankind is best served where the self-regarding instincts are encouraged rather than thwarted. As Lord Samuel, discussing the value of self-interest, has written: [42]

> Here we may find an additional cause of the loosening hold of religion, and of the perplexity of our times that has followed. For the modern mind, looking at the whole matter afresh, without feeling bound by traditional orthodoxies, sees that morality, if it is to be comprehensive, must allow that egoism, at proper times and in proper measure, is a right motive, that it is indeed essential to welfare. When religion seems to ignore or to contradict this, common sense and religion stand opposed.

In a notorious speech, the late Lord Birkenhead put the objection in far more extreme form:

> The school of idealism is the very antithesis of the school of self-interest. And yet nothing is more apparent than that politically, economically and philosophically the motive of self-interest not only is but must be and ought to be the mainspring of human conduct. . . . The world continues to offer glittering prizes to those who have stout hearts and glittering swords.

And there are theological difficulties, too, in the idea of disinterested service of God. Only a few mystics, and these in a very restricted sense, have suggested that God *needs* man's worship.[43] The Infinite Being who lacks nothing has no needs. Man was created for his good, not for God's. These

---

[42] *Belief and Action,* revised ed., Lond., Cassell, 1953, p. 90.
[43] See especially the lengthy discussion in Isaiah Horovitz's *Shene Luhoth Ha-Berith* (*Sheloh*) (Amsterdam, 1649), 10 *Ma'amaroth, Ma'amar* III and IV.

are the general postulates of higher religion. Why then should it be right for man to serve God without thought of self and so suggest that God needs his worship? To put these objections crudely – may not the frank self-seeker, pursuing the right aims, do more good, more effectively, than the tortured saint morbidly engaged in the stultifying task of 'purifying' his motives?

But to take these objections too seriously is to question not alone the ideal of disinterestedness but of the love of God and, indeed, of the whole Theistic position. No theologian could suggest that God 'needs' our worship in any crude, direct, or anthropomorphic sense. But the doctrine taught in one form or another by all the great religious thinkers, that God created man because it is part of His nature, to give of His goodness and to share that goodness with His creatures, implies that, in an indirect sense, God needs man's worship if only because man needs to worship in order to share in God's goodness. Or, to put this in another way, to serve the Highest and to participate in God's purpose is man's supreme privilege. So that, if God wants man to fulfil himself, God must want man, to serve and worship Him. Disinterested service by man is the way in which he shares God's love. It is the way in which he becomes God-like by giving of himself without thought of reward. Disinterestedness is a turning of the mind outwards. It is a reaching out for the divine, a broadening of one's horizon, an enlargement of one's vision in the name of the Source of all enlargement. 'Out of my straits I called upon the Lord; He answered me with great enlargement.'[44] Self-interest, on the other hand, if carried too far, is a turning of the mind on itself. It is both the product and the cause of narrowness of mind and outlook. It is the imprisonment of the self in the fetters of the consuming ego.

As for the charge that disinterestedness is stultifying, a hindrance to effective action, this is frequently true. Certainly

[44] Ps. cxviii, 5.

too much self-examination can be exceedingly harmful, as some of the adherents of the austere Lithuanian *Musar* movement learned to their cost. It cannot be healthy always to be analysing one's motives and it does not require great psychological acumen to recognise that the introspective person can be a self-seeker. Man is compared to a tree, observed a *Hasidic* teacher with keener insight, for just as the tree grows imperceptibly, a man should not be too fond of peering inwards anxiously to watch his spiritual growth. But when all has been said, the lives of the great saints of every faith testify to the tremendous vitality of the truly sincere and dedicated personality. Disinterestedness has its power, too, and, in the lives of its best representatives, it is a power wedded to a calm wisdom unhampered by clouding passion.

In this connection, William James's analysis of the saintly character[45] is to the point. James speaks of 'the expulsive power of a higher affection'. The indulgent woman, for example, can toil without an instant of complaint when she becomes a mother and is possessed by maternal excitement.[46] James rightly distinguishes between the man who deliberately chooses to overcome his fears and inhibitions and the genius who does not feel them at all.[47] Given, he argues, a sufficient amount of love, indignation, generosity, magnanimity, the whole mass of cowardly obstructions sink away at once.[48] When these obstructions vanish there is a bright quality to life especially when the controlling emotion is religious.[49] 'The true monk takes nothing with him but his lyre.' One is reminded of the role of *simhah* – 'joy' – in *Hasidic* life and thought. It is true that saintly behaviour frequently appears unattractive, even repellent, to the outsider but such

[45] *The Varieties of Religious Experience*, 1903, Lectures XI, XII and XIII, pp. 259-315 and Lectures XIV and XV, pp. 326-378.
[46] Ibid. p. 262.
[47] p. 265.
[48] p. 266.
[49] p. 267.

behaviour cannot be appreciated by the detached observer. As James concludes: [60]

> But in all these matters of sentiment one must have 'been there' one's self in order to understand them. . . . One can never fathom an emotion or divine its dictates by standing outside of it. In the glowing hour of excitement, however, all incomprehensibilities are solved, and what was so enigmatical from without becomes transparently obvious.

Granted that disinterestedness is desirable is it possible of attainment? Can a man truly forget himself? There are obvious examples of self-interest masquerading as disinterestedness. There is the person who, aware how easily the self-seeker is found out, resolves to lead a disinterested life but his true motive is to win the esteem of others. Or, there is the person who strives for disinterestedness in order to feel superior to the common herd in whom the motive of self-regard predominates. Knowing as we do that an element of self-interest enters into all our thoughts and acts – how even the advocacy of disinterestedness may be a particularly obnoxious form of it – are we not justified in questioning whether the saints were not deluding themselves?

Perhaps disinterestedness can never be more than an ideal to which one can only hope to approximate, a position to be gained rather than one permanently held. Bahya Ibn Pakudah indeed suggests that a purely altruistic act is impossible for man. Bahya[61] distinguishes between God's love which is entirely disinterested and man's love in which a measure of self-interest is always present. The father who benefits his son does so because the son is part of himself, the substance of his hope and ambition. Charity given by the rich in order to win the reward of Heaven can be compared to the businessman who gives a small good immediately in the hope of purchasing an advantage in the future. People who help each other for the sake of love and praise and honour and worldly

[60] p. 325.
[61] *The Duties of the Heart*, Gate of Divine Service, Introduction.

reward can be compared to the man who gives his neighbour goods to take care of until he wants them for himself. Even the rich man who takes pity on the poor and afflicted, whose sufferings are painful to him, can be compared to one who heals himself of a painful illness, for when he gives to alleviate their suffering he intends to relieve himself of a pain that afflicts his soul. Thus, while Bahya praises even the self-motivated good deed his is the 'Utilitarian' view that the primary intention of everyone in doing good to others, is to do good to himself or to save himself from pain.

Hayyim of Volozhyn's (1749-1821) *Nephesh Ha-Hayyim*[52] contains a detailed exposition of our theme. The book was written as a counterblast to the *Hasidim* who frequently argued that their opponents had completely set aside the *lishmah* ideal. The author naturally quotes the 'realistic' saying of Rab Judah in the name of Rab (d. 247 C.E.) that a man should always occupy himself with *Torah* and good deeds though it is not for their own sake for, out of doing good with an ulterior motive, there comes doing good for its own sake.[53] When Rab speaks of pure service *coming* from service with an ulterior motive his meaning is not, argues Hayyim of Volozhyn, that a gradual transformation takes place in the character of the self-motivated man so that one morning he will wake up to find himself behaving disinterestedly. Human nature does not function in so mechanical a fashion, there is an ebb and flow in the life of the spirit. The meaning is rather that whatever a man's original motive for carrying out the good deed, he forgets it in the performance of the deed and rejoices in doing good for its own sake.[54] Some of

[52] Vilna, 1824.

[53] Pes. 50b.

[54] *Nephesh Ha-Hayyim,* Portion between *Sha'ar* III and IV, Chapter 3. Cf. the same work, *Sha'ar* IV, Chapter 3, for the defence of the older rabbinic view that the ideal of 'Torah for its own sake' (*Torah lishmah*) is to be taken literally and not that the student should cleave to God during his studies (*debhekvth*), as the
(*Continued at foot of p. 72*)

the *Hasidic* teachers, too, were aware of this distinction, as the following anecdote shows. The *Besht* is said to have gazed enraptured at the performance of a tight-rope walker for, he remarked, although the man is paid to risk his life, at the moment he crosses on the rope he does not think of his fee but only of the task in hand, otherwise he would fall to his death!

Maimonides, on the other hand, dealing with this question believes that by engaging in many forms of worthy activity it is inevitable that *some* of them, at least, will be free from any selfish motive. This is the basis of Maimonides' 'Neo-Platonic' and therefore anachronistic interpretation of Hananiah ben Akashya's famous saying:

> The Holy One, Blessed is He, was minded to grant merit to Israel; therefore hath He multiplied for them the *Torah* and commandments:[55] It is one of the fundamental principles of faith in the *Torah* that when a man fulfils one of the six hundred and thirteen precepts in a fit and proper manner without associating any worldly motive whatsoever but doing it for its own sake out of love, as I have explained to you, by virtue of this he merits the life of the World to Come. Concerning this, R. Hananiah said that seeing that the precepts of the *Torah* are so numerous, it is impossible for a man during his lifetime not to do one of them in a proper manner and with the right intention and by performing this precept he revives his soul.[56]

There is, too, the question of degree to be considered. It may well be that no man is *entirely* free from self-interest. 'For there is not a just man on earth that doeth good, and sinneth not'[57] was interpreted by the *Besht* to mean 'and

Hasidim taught. To attempt this latter, argues the author, is to fail in *Torah* study, for concentrated study is impossible without undivided attention to the subject studied! If the student thoroughly immerses himself in the legal discussions on fraud, for instance, in order to master the *Halakhah,* he cannot in the process be aware of God.

[55] *Mishnah*, Makk. III, 16.
[56] Comment. to Makk. ad loc.
[57] Eccl. vii, 20.

sinneth not in the good which he does' i.e. no man can be entirely free from self-interest in anything he does. But man desires to give as well as to receive, he possesses altruistic, as well as egoistic, instincts so that the ideal of disinterestedness may not demand complete forgetfulness of self but that greater play be given to the altruistic instincts when doing good.

No one would wish to deny the difficulty of disinterestedness. Traditional Jewish teaching would certainly not encourage its followers to desist from doing good because their motives are not of the purest. It believes, it has so often been said with truth, in the healing power of the *deed*. But, in that teaching, the ideal of 'for the sake of Heaven' is never lost sight of, the ideal of the Psalmist: 'To do Thy will is my desire, O my God.' True the fundamentalist or the man of naïve, unquestioning faith finds it easier to follow this ideal. But can the more sophisticated believer afford to neglect the ideal without depriving his religious faith of all its inwardness and spiritual power?

V

THE SANCTIFICATION OF THE NAME

S IMEON BEN SHETAH (1st cent. C.E.), one of the most
important of the Pharisaic teachers, it is said, found a
precious stone of great value hanging around the neck of a
donkey he had bought from an Arab. Refusing to yield to
the entreaties of his disciples, who urged him to keep the
treasure God had sent him, he returned the stone, saying, 'I
bought a donkey, not a precious stone.' The Arab witness
to the Sage's integrity thereupon exclaimed: 'Blessed is the
God of Simeon ben Shetah.'[1] This story is frequently quoted
in Jewish literature as an illustration of the doctrine of
Kiddush Ha-Shem (the sanctification of the Name) a doctrine
derived from the verse: 'And ye shall not profane My holy
name; but I will be hallowed among the children of Israel: I
am the Lord who hallow you.'[2, 3]

God's name becomes hallowed when those who love Him
act in such a manner that it is evident that their belief has
had a transforming effect on their lives. Simeon ben Shetah
would not have endangered his reputation if he had decided
to keep the stone. There was no kind of social pressure to
compel him to restore the stone to its owner. Far from any
social blame being attached to Simeon for keeping it, to
many, including Simeon's disciples, this seemed the prudent
thing to do. And prudence is not usually slow in finding its
justification on grounds of principle. 'God had given him

[1] Tal.J. B.M. ii, 5, 8c, Deut. R. iii, 3.
[2] Lev. xxii, 32.
[3] Siphra to Lev. xxii, 32, ed. Weiss, p. 99b and freq.

a treasure.' But the God Simeon worshipped would not allow him to act dishonestly. In returning the stone Simeon demonstrated that belief in God and obedience to His will are no unworthy manifestations of credulity, no 'profane' ideas but 'holy', life-challenging and life-transforming, moving men to say: 'If this is what faith means then faith is worth the having.'

It is for this reason that martyrdom is known in the Jewish tradition as *Kiddush Ha-Shem*. The martyr demonstrates that for one man, at least, religious faith is real. The most subtle acts of charity, the most self-denying religious practices, the most intense mortifications of the flesh, all may be indulged in as a means to self-assertion or self-aggrandizement. They do not necessarily testify to a self-transcending faith. The man who fasts or the wearer of a hair-shirt may be getting a bigger thrill out of the knowledge that men admire his extraordinary sanctity than he would have obtained from his food and his comforts. There is no evidence that he is prepared to give of his life in the worship of his God, only that he prefers one kind of life to another. But when life itself is offered on the altar of faith then men see that somewhere on earth belief is meaningful, that God has really possessed one man's inner life. The martyr's sacrifice is not in itself evidence of truth, for all faiths have their martyrs and people have given their lives for contradictory ideals. But apart from the very rare case of the self-seeking martyr (there are people who like to think of the posthumous fame that will be theirs and allow their minds to dwell on the tributes that will be paid to their memory) this thing is attested to by martyrdom that belief is not false, that all who bear the name of God upon their lips are not bent on fooling others. One man's faith has been vindicated. For one man, at least, religion is not 'opium for the people'. This man's sacrifice has rendered less suspect the religious protestations of all men. Though many who profess religion may be hypocrites, the martyr shows that religion is not synonymous with hypocrisy. He has sanctified God's name.

It is Israel's privilege to bear *God's name*. However the doctrine of the Chosen People is understood it involves the responsibility of Israel to live in a manner that will bring glory to the Name. It is not Israel's honour that is at stake, however, but the honour of God. Israel behaves 'differently', in order to make God's name known among the children of men. 'Not unto us, O Lord, not unto us, but unto thy Name give glory, for thy lovingkindness and for thy truth's sake.'[4] Richard Braithwaite, the seventeenth century author of *English Gentleman and English Gentlewoman*, writes:

> In every deed there is no ornament which adds more lustre to a gentleman than to be humbly-minded, being as low in conceit as he is high in place. The gentleman scorns pride as a derogation of Gentry.[5]

The Jewish gentleman, the devotee of *Kiddush Ha-Shem*, scorns pride, and other faults of character, as a derogation of God.

But the doctrine of *Kiddush Ha-Shem* possesses a far deeper significance than attestation to the power of religious faith. The profound implication of the doctrine is that in a sense God *needs* man for His purpose to be fulfilled. We have noted this idea in the previous chapter. Here is the place to consider it in somewhat greater detail. Religious thinkers have drawn a distinction between God as He is in Himself and God as He is revealed to man. It is the task of the historian of religious ideas to show how this concept has been expounded in the writings of theologians of many different schools, Jewish and non-Jewish, and to trace the various forms it has assumed. For our purpose it will be sufficient to consider in simplified form what the distinction between God as He is in Himself and God as He is revealed means and to note the bearing of this distinction on the doctrine of *Kiddush*

[4] Ps. cxv, 1.

[5] See Harold Nicolson: *Good Behaviour*, Lond., Constable, 1955, p. 191.

THE SANCTIFICATION OF THE NAME

Ha-Shem. It is generally accepted by Theists that God is so far above man that His essence is utterly beyond man's comprehension. And yet there must be some point of contact between God and man otherwise the great ideas of prayer and worship, obedience and religious discipline, consecration and holiness, faith and trust, common to all Theistic faiths, are meaningless. The distinction is drawn, therefore, between God as He is in Himself and God as He is revealed to man, between (in the words of Pascal) the God of the philosophers and the God of Abraham, Isaac and Jacob. God as He is in Himself cannot be known to man. We can only know God through his manifestations in the Universe. It is God as He reveals Himself to man who is the God of religion. It follows from this that the recognition of God by man makes God, as it were, real for man. The recognition of God by man is far more than the acceptance of that which is there. It becomes *there* as a result of the recognition. It is man by his dedicated life who makes the hidden God into the God of religion. This is the deeper significance of *Kiddush Ha-Shem.* Heroic religious living, stemming from deep faith, brings God down from Heaven as a power in men's lives. There is an oft-quoted *Midrash* which appears to give expression to this thought. Commenting on the verse in Isaiah: 'Ye are My witnesses, saith the Lord, and I am God'[6] a second century teacher remarked: 'If ye are My witnesses then I am God, but if ye are not My witnesses then I am not God, as it were.'[7] This is to say that a witness is no more than one who testifies to certain events having taken place. He has no necessary part in those events. If this is the kind of witness meant in the verse the order should have been reversed: 'I am God and ye are My witnesses': first the 'event' and then the testimony.

[6] Is. xliii, 12.
[7] *Yalkut,* Is. 454. Cf. the interpretation given here of the verse: 'Unto Thee I lift up mine eyes, O thou that art enthroned in the heavens' (Ps. cxxiii, 1) – 'Without me Thou would'st not be enthroned in the heavens'!

But the witness spoken of by the prophet, in the opinion of the Rabbinic teacher, is one who not alone testifies to the event but one who makes it happen. The situation we call 'confronted by God' is created by the act of testifying. Attestation, here, must precede that which is given!

This point is well made in a stimulating essay by Hugo Bergmann entitled 'The Hallowing of the Name' with the suggestive sub-title 'God depends on Man, as Man on God'.[*] In the Jewish conception, says Bergmann, *'God's destiny hangs upon the world's outcome.'* 'God is, to his creatures, a task to be fulfilled, an end to be realised.' It must be remarked that this must in no way be interpreted that God is constantly 'emerging' in the sense that a thinker like Samuel Alexander uses the term. Bergmann rightly emphasises this:

> For there can be no mistake about it: to dissolve the idea of God into that of a goal, to think of God merely as a *telos* to be realised – that would be to miss the Jewish conception of God completely. That God is, independently of whether or not I realise him within myself, is not a subject for doubt to the Jew. But – and this is the decisive turn of thought which the Jew contemplates – God exists only for himself, he is not something existing in himself that one can grasp from without, that can be possessed in the sense that a thing is grasped. Thus, he exists only for those who are in communion with him, who are in union with him. Hence the Jew asks: in what way *is* God for me? And he answers: insofar as he becomes my *act* in my life. Insofar as I have validated him, has he become a reality in my world.

Perhaps in the English translation of Bergmann's essay the thought is not brought out as clearly as one would wish. It may be paraphrased in this way. When Jewish tradition speaks of God *depending* on man this means not that God as He is in Himself depends on man but that God as He is revealed depends on man. In the above-mentioned Rabbinic quotation on the *witnessing* to God the Hebrew word *kebheyakhol* 'as it were' (the usual Rabbinic qualification

[*] *Commentary*, March, 1952, p. 271f, translated by Felix Giovanelli.

78

introduced whenever anything particularly bold is postulated of God) is highly significant. God *as it were* depends on man, i.e. in *reality* He is not so dependent. The nature of the dependence of the revealed God on man is that God has His purpose for man in the world and He has given man freedom of choice. Consequently, He has delivered, as it were, His purpose into the hands of man.

It cannot be denied that there is a grandeur in the idea, found in various modern philosophies of nature, which recognises a certain teleological character in the universe and which thinks of man as helping to fulfil nature's purpose. But the refusal of some of these philosophies to attribute this teleological character to Creative Mind makes them unacceptable to the Theist apart from the inherent difficulty they possess of failing to account for the existence of a 'purpose' in 'blind' nature. The doctrine of *Kiddush Ha-Shem* allows us to have the best of both worlds. All the grandeur of the concept of man having the destiny of the universe in his hands is preserved without the fear that this is to attribute purpose to a blind process which can have no purpose. In poetic fashion Martin Buber has described the Kabbalistic notion that God and His Divine Presence (the *Shekhina*) can be 'united' by the acts of man:

> God is divided into two, through the created world and its actions. He is divided into the ultimate being of God, Elohut, which is remote and apart from the creatures, and the Presence of God, his Glory, the Shekhina, which dwells in the world, wandering astray and scattered. Redemption alone will unite both for Eternity. But it is the property of the soul of man, by means of service, to bring the Shekhina nearer to its source, and to let it re-enter into it. In this instant of homecoming, before it must descend into the being of the world, the whirlpool which howls in the life of the stars is hushed, the torches of the great desolation are extinguished, the lash in the hand of fate is lowered, and the pain of the world is stilled and listens: the grace of graces has appeared, and blessing pours down into space, till the powers of entanglement begin to drag down the Glory again, and all is as before.

79

Victor Gollancz, in his remarkable anthology *A Year of Grace*, quotes this interpretation of Buber together with many similar passages from the writings of mystics and philosophers in which the same mood is expressed.[9] But by including the following passage from the work of Samuel Alexander, Gollancz is suggesting that the mystical idea of God *needing* man is akin to the notion of an emergent deity. Alexander writes:

> Accordingly, in its relation to conduct, religion does not so much command us to perform our duties with the consciousness that they are the commands of God, as rather it is religion to do our duty with the consciousness of helping to create his deity.

No Theist would speak of 'helping to create his deity'. But many have spoken of man 'helping' God by making His Presence felt in the world. It is this latter idea that is behind the doctrine of *Kiddush Ha-Shem*.

Just as *Kiddush Ha-Shem* is among the highest values of Judaism its opposite *Hillul Ha-Shem,* the profanation of God's name, is among the most grievous faults of which a Jew can be guilty. Even an unintentional profanation of the Name is said to be sin.[10] In Rabbinic teaching the act which brings about *Hillul Ha-Shem* need not be an offence in itself but if it has the effect of lowering the standard of religion and morality *Hillul Ha-Shem* results. Thus, one Talmudic teacher said that if he buys meat from the butcher without paying for it immediately it is a *Hillul Ha-Shem*[11] for the faintest breath of suspicion that a scholar is lax in discharging his debts is sufficient for this offence to be committed. Another teacher said that if he walks four cubits without his *Tephillin* and without concentration on the *Torah* a *Hillul Ha-Shem* results.[12] When a *Hillul Ha-Shem* is being assessed

[9] *A Year of Grace – Passages Chosen and Arranged to Express a Mood About God and Man,* Lond., Gollancz, 1950, Second Part III, p. 133f.
[10] 'Aboth IV, 4.
[11] Yom. 86a.
[12] Yom. ibid.

it is not the legality of an action that is in dispute but the type of character it displays in its perpetrator. An action may be innocent in itself but if the result of such an action is to suggest that the demands of religion or morality are not being taken seriously a *Hillul Ha-Shem* is perpetrated. The follower of *Torah* must so conduct himself that it is evident to all that the *Torah* has had a beneficial effect on his character. As the Rabbis put it:

> If someone studies Scripture and *Mishnah,* and attends on the disciples of the wise, is honest in business, and speaks pleasantly to others, what do people say concerning him? 'Happy the father who taught him *Torah,* happy the teacher who taught him *Torah;* woe unto people who have not studied the *Torah;* for this man has studied the *Torah* – look how fine his ways are, how righteous his deeds.' Of him does Scripture say: *And He said unto me: Thou art My servant Israel, in whom I will be glorified.*[13] But if someone studies Scripture and *Mishnah,* attends on disciples of the wise, but is dishonest in business, and discourteous in his relations with others, what do people say about him? 'Woe unto him who studied the *Torah,* woe unto his father who taught him *Torah;* woe unto the teacher who taught him *Torah!* This man studied the *Torah*: look how corrupt his deeds, how ugly his ways!' Of him Scripture says: *In that men said of them: These are the people of the Lord, and are come forth out of His land.*[14] [15]

In line with the same teaching R. Israel Salanter once said that *he* knew he was no great scholar and saint but seeing that, for his sins, people looked upon him as such it was his duty to live up to the reputation he had acquired otherwise he would be guilty of *Hillul Ha-Shem.*

Kiddush Ha-Shem means, as we have seen, helping God to fulfil His purpose; *Hillul Ha-Shem* means some frustration of that purpose. Whenever it is publicly demonstrated that the forces of evil are gaining ground held by the forces of good

[13] Is. xlix, 3.
[14] Ezek. xxxvi, 20.
[15] Yom. ibid.

there is *Hillul Ha-Shem*. A bold expression of this idea is given by the second century teacher, R. Meir, in an interpretation of the verse in Deuteronomy: [16]

> And if a man have committed a sin worthy of death, and he be put to death, and thou hang him on a tree; his body shall not remain all night upon the tree, but thou shalt surely bury him the same day; for he that is hanged is a reproach unto God. . . .

What is meant, asks R. Meir, by 'he that is hanged is a reproach unto God'? He replies with a parable. A certain great king had a twin brother who resembled him in form and features. This brother was a hardened criminal who was eventually caught and hanged for his crime. Seeing that he resembled the king an order was given for him to be removed from the gibbet that people should not say: the king is hanging! [17] Man is created in the image of God. When he is guilty of sin it is a reproach to God in whose image he is created.

An objection to the whole doctrine of *Kiddush Ha-Shem* may be raised on the grounds that the doctrine panders to the opportunist mood. If it is not so much the right or wrong of an act which counts but the impression it makes on others does this not leave the door wide open for an attitude of expediency? Is it not sound religious teaching which urges that man should be conscious of his responsibilities to God and not to men in living the good life? To say, as the doctrine of *Kiddush Ha-Shem* appears to say, that the impression on others is what counts is to encourage the man who does the right thing with a sharp eye on the main chance and refrains from doing wrong in obedience to what has been called cynically, the eleventh commandment: 'Do not be found out!'

But to understand *Kiddush Ha-Shem* in this way is to fail to grasp its meaning. It is not the honour or the reputation of man that is at stake but the honour and reputation of God.

[16] xxi, 22-23.
[17] *Yalkut*, Deut. ad loc. 530.

THE SANCTIFICATION OF THE NAME

Man must think of the impression his deeds make on others not in order to bolster up his own esteem but to encourage others to live the good life. There is an abundance of Jewish teaching on the need for adherence to truth even where this adherence results in condemnation by others. Indeed some Jewish teachers have gone to the extreme of suggesting that the God-fearing man is completely indifferent to human praise or blame.[18] And the old folk-motif of the thirty-six hidden righteous men in whose merit the world endures reminds us of the value of 'hidden' virtue. All this is in no way incompatible with the advocacy of *Kiddush Ha-Shem* and the struggle against *Hillul Ha-Shem*. For these doctrines assert that man has responsibilities to others, stemming from his responsibility to God, which should make him wish to set a good example and refrain from setting a bad example; not to further his own interests but to increase God's glory. Hidden virtue is itself a means of glorifying God. But there are occasions when the power of example must be evoked. To quote once again Israel Salanter:

> Nowadays, when Judaism is attacked on many fronts, I fail to see how there can be any 'hidden righteous men' for if they are truly good men how can they remain 'hidden'!

Jewish teaching is emphatic that hiding one's virtues is one thing,[19] parading one's vices a very different thing.[20]

[18] This idea is found in the mediaeval sources. A *Hasidic* interpretation of Ps. xvi, 8 'I have set the Lord always before me . . .' notes that the first Hebrew word in the verse – *shivithi* – can mean (though ungrammatically) 'all is equal to me' i.e. whether I am praised or blamed. The verse is thus made to yield the thought: 'It is the same to me whether I am praised or blamed by men because the Lord is always before me.'

[19] See Sukk. 49b: ' "And to walk humbly with thy God" (Micah vi, 8) refers to attending funerals and dowering a bride for her wedding. Now can we not make a deduction from the less to the greater: for if in matters which are normally performed publicly the *Torah* says: "Walk humbly", on things which are usually done unobtrusively, how very much more!'

[20] See foot of page 84.

Moreover it is not sufficient for wrong not to be done; it must be seen not to have been done. The verse in Numbers:[21] 'Then ye shall be clear before the Lord, *and before Israel....*' was interpreted by the Rabbis to include a whole set of actions which, though not wrong in themselves, must be avoided because they give the *appearance* of wrong having been done.[22] It is for this reason, too, that a *public* desecration of the Sabbath is considered in traditional Jewish teaching to be a far more serious offence than private desecration.[23]

Kiddush Ha-Shem follows from acts which demonstrate that religion is being sincerely lived. *Hillul Ha-Shem* results from acts which demonstrate that the burden of religious responsibility sits lightly on a person. The question of the rightness or wrongness of the act in itself is not here the salient factor, as we have seen, but whether it is calculated to

[20] This helps to place in its proper perspective the strange passage in the Talmud which runs: 'R. Illai the elder said: "If a man sees that his passion gets the better of him, let him go to a place where he is unknown, let him clothe himself in black, and let him do what his heart asks, but do not let him profane the name of God publicly"' (Hag. 16a). Certainly this was never interpreted in Jewish traditional teaching as permission to sin in secret. Joseph S. Bloch in his *Israel and the Nations*, Berlin, 1927, discusses this passage at length (p. 316f.) with insight into its correct meaning.

[21] Num. xxxii, 22.

[22] See Pes. *Mishnah*, IV, 1-5, Betz, 9a and very freq.

[23] Hull. 5a and freq. There is, however, one Talmudic passage from which it would appear that a public crime is to be preferred to one committed in private: 'The disciples of R. Johanan b. Zakkai asked him why the *Torah* was more severe on a thief (who steals in secret) than a robber (who steals openly). He replied: The robber puts the honour of the slave on the same level as the honour of his owner, whereas the thief does not put the honour of the slave on the same level as the honour of his master for, as it were, he acts as if the eye of Below would not be seeing and the ear of Below would not be hearing. . . . R. Meir said: The

(*Continued on p. 85*)

increase or decrease the respect men have for religion. It is
for this reason that representative Jewish teachers have con-
sistently admonished Jews to preserve the very highest
standards of commercial integrity. Even practices not in themselves unlawful should be rejected if they give the impression
of dishonesty or lack of integrity. The Jew bears God's name
and his obligation is to bring honour to God by offering Him
an honourable life. The strain of living under such a burden
is severe but nothing less is demanded of those who would
adhere to the ideal of *Kiddush Ha-Shem*.

following parable is reported in the name of R. Gamaliel. What
do the thief and the robber resemble? Two people who dwelt
in one town and held banquets. One invited the townspeople
and did not invite the royal family, the other invited neither the
townspeople nor the royal family. Which deserves the heavier
punishment? Surely the one who invited the townspeople but did
not invite the royal family' (B.K. 79b). It is possible that a distinction is made in Rabbinic thought on this matter between
religious and ethical offences. The religious offence, i.e. the
profanation of the Sabbath, is no offence against society. As an
offence against God it is greater when committed in public for
then there is public affront to God's honour. But the ethical
offence is one against society as well as against God and the man
who is afraid of the condemnation of society without being
afraid of the condemnation of God deserves greater censure than
the man who fears the condemnation of neither!

VI

TRUST IN GOD

THE Hebrew term generally used for trust in God, *Bittahon,* is found frequently in the Bible in this and in many other forms.[1] The root *batah* appears to mean in kindred languages 'to throw down upon his face'.[2] The association of ideas is 'throwing firmly down', 'resting securely' and then 'trust' and 'confidence'. The word is used in the panegyric on the virtuous woman who is reliable so that 'the heart of her husband *trusteth* in her'.[3] In a number of Biblical passages the word is found in conjunction with a word meaning 'to be quiet'.[4] The mood expressed in these passages is one of quiet confidence. The man of *Bittahon* is possessed of the assurance that his life is in God's hands and that therefore he has nothing to fear. The classic example of this steadfast faith is the declaration of Jeremiah:

> Blessed is the man that trusteth in the Lord, And whose trust the Lord is. For he shall be as a tree planted by the waters, And that spreadeth out its roots by the river, And shall not see when heat cometh, But its foliage shall be luxuriant; And shall not be anxious in the year of drought, Neither shall cease from yielding fruit.[5]

[1] Eccl. ix, 4, II Kings xviii, 19, Is. xxxvi, 4, Zeph. iii, 2, Ps. xxviii, 7, xxxi, 7, lii, 10, lvi, 5 and 12, cxix, 42, cxliii, 8, and very freq.
[2] B.D.B. s.v. *batah.*
[3] Prov. xxxi, 11.
[4] Root *shakat,* Judg. xviii, 7 and 27, Ezek. xxxviii, 11, Is. xxx, 15 and xxxii, 17.
[5] Jer. xvii, 7-8.

TRUST IN GOD

Jeremiah's faith is paralleled by that of the Psalmist:

> Put not your trust in princes, Nor in the son of man, in whom there is no help. His breath goeth forth, he returneth to his dust; In that very day his thoughts perish. Happy is he whose help is the God of Jacob, Whose hope is in the Lord his God.[6]

Trust in God does not mean confidence that all one's undertakings will prosper. *Bittahon* is far removed from undue sanguinity about the future or naïve Micawberism. In Jewish teaching it is not advocated as a substitute for honest toil and effort. The popular saying: 'God helps those who help themselves' has often been used as an excuse for the cynical attempt to eliminate the divine from human affairs and as *carte blanche* for the disregard of religious restraints but for all that the saying is not without its truth. Trusting in God is not incompatible with keeping the powder dry. The Rabbis quote the verse: 'And the Lord thy God will bless thee *in all that thou doest*'[7] as justification, if such were needed, from the religious point of view, for human striving.[8] When the second century teacher, R. Simeon b. Yohai, taught that the man who did God's will could afford to neglect his material responsibilities and God would provide, his contemporary, R. Ishmael, quoted the verse: 'That thou mayest gather in thy corn'[9] to show that human effort can never be dispensed with.[10] A later master observed that many had tried to follow R. Simeon's teaching without success but many had followed R. Ishmael's teaching and their efforts had prospered.[11] It is important to see this debate against its background. Both R. Simeon and R. Ishmael lived in the period which followed the wars with Rome. As a result of these wars and the sporadic attempts at revolt by the Jews the land was devastated. The whole economic position of Palestinian Jewry

[6] Ps. cxlvi, 3-5.
[7] Deut. xv, 18.
[8] *Siphre, Re'eh,* sec. 123.
[9] Deut. xi, 14.
[10] *Siphre, 'Ekebh* sec. 42, Ber. 35b.
[11] Ber. ibid.

had deteriorated so that the Rabbinic literature produced in this period shows little evidence of extended trade or commerce. R. Simeon himself, we are told, was obliged to flee his home because of his outspokenness on Roman oppression.[12] Against such a background it is not difficult to understand R. Simeon's view. It has been said that the Jew in the Ghetto had nowhere to turn so he was obliged to go upwards! Something like this must have been behind R. Simeon's statement. In a world which offered little hope for material prosperity it was natural for a great Jewish teacher to urge his flock not to think of the morrow but to devote all their energies to the *Torah* in the belief that God would provide. Legend has it that when R. Simeon came out of the cave in which he had lived the life of a hermit for many years, he saw people ploughing and reaping and was distressed that Jews were 'forsaking eternal life to engage in temporal affairs'. The gaze of the holy man burned into annihilation the crops and the farmers. Whereupon a heavenly voice proceeded to declare: 'Is it to destroy my world that you have come? Return to your cave!'[13] The authors of this legend were clearly expressing their disapproval of R. Simeon's attitude. The same disapproval was voiced in his own day by R. Ishmael. But both opinions are recorded in the Talmud and the Talmud enjoys an authority second only to the Bible for Jews. Consequently, though from the historical point of view both R. Simeon and R. Ishmael were reacting to a definite situation at one point of time, the debate is always quoted in subsequent Jewish discussions on the relationship between trust in God and human effort. Many Jewish teachers have sided with R. Ishmael, others have sided with R. Simeon.

The religious mind is powerfully attracted by the 'extreme' view of R. Simeon and tends to be repelled by the 'common sense' view of R. Ishmael. For many religious people faith is to be approached in a spirit of adventure, it is 'holy folly' and

[12] Sabb. 33b.
[13] Sabb. ibid.

the very opposite of a cold, calculating approach to life. When the 'leap of faith' has been taken the religious man does not want to feel that he is the arbiter of his destiny. He wants to leave everything to God. He tends to look upon R. Ishmael's view as too comfortably 'bourgeois', as a too humdrum doctrine out of keeping with the response required of one whose soul has been touched by the Absolute. A good example of the protest against R. Ishmael's opinion (or, better, a re-interpretation of it) is to be found in the writing of a fine thinker of the old school, Rabbi E. Dessler. Dessler, in his posthumous work, *Mikhtabh Me-Elijahu*,[14] devotes a section to an acute analysis of the meaning of *Bittahon* and its relation to human strivings. I believe that Dessler's views are one-sided and that they fail to do justice to many significant areas of modern life. But it would be helpful if his views were fairly stated before the attempt is made to refute them.

Dessler begins by quoting the Midrashic interpretation of: 'And the Lord God took the man, and put him into the Garden of Eden to work it and to keep it.'[15] This, says, the *Midrash,* cannot be taken literally for the garden was watered naturally and the trees produced fruit of their own accord. 'To work it' means 'to study the *Torah*' and 'to keep it' means 'to keep the precepts of the *Torah*'.[16] Human toil was unknown in the Garden of Eden. It was decreed as a punishment for Adam's eating of the forbidden fruit. Labour is a curse and though man must labour in obedience to the divine will he should indulge in it as little as possible devoting his main efforts to the study and practice of the *Torah*. This means, for Dessler, in the various kinds of spiritual activity it is the privilege of the *Torah* student to undertake. Dessler in support of this attitude quotes from Moses Hayyim Luzzatto's definition of *Bittahon*:

One should cast one's burden upon the Lord, in the knowledge

[14] Lond. 1955.
[15] Gen. ii, 15.
[16] *Yalkut,* Gen. 22.

that no man is deprived of what has been apportioned to him. As our Sages said: 'How much a man should obtain for his sustenance is fixed during the Days of Penitence, between *Rosh Ha-Shanah* and *Yom Kippur*.'[17] Or, as they say elsewhere, 'No man can deprive his neighbour of that which has been apportioned to him, even to the extent of a hair's breadth.'[18] In fact, the amount of sustenance allotted to each man would be granted to him even if he sat idle, were it not for the primeval curse expressed in the words, 'By the sweat of thy brow thou shalt eat bread.'[19] Therefore must man put forth effort to obtain a livelihood; for thus did the Most High decree, and this exertion is a levied tribute which mankind cannot escape paying. . . . But it is not really the effort that counts, though that effort is indispensable; in putting it forth a man does his duty. Nevertheless, a man may enjoy the blessing of Heaven without spending all his days in strenuous labour. . . . The true way is that of the saints of old who made the study of the *Torah* their principal occupation and their worldly calling secondary, thereby doing justice to both. When a man has done some work he should leave the rest to God, and not be worried concerning worldly matters. Only then are his mind and heart in a condition to cultivate saintliness and perfect piety.[20]

Following this line of thought, Dessler suggests that the extent of human effort required depends on how far such effort succeeds in screening from view what otherwise would be a miracle. After Adam's sin man is not worthy of having miracles performed for him daily. He is obliged to engage in the endeavour to feed and clothe himself and his family in order that God's blessing may be attributed to the human effort rather than to miraculous divine intervention. But the man of faith sees, in fact, only the miracle and looks upon his own efforts as having no more effect that the screening of the miracle from view. The example is quoted of R. Zundel Salanter, an early nineteenth century saint, who said that he

[17] Betz. 16a.
[18] Yom. 38b.
[19] Gen. iii, 19.
[20] *Mesillat Yesharim*, ed. Kaplan, Chapter 21, pp. 190-192.

fulfils the duty of human effort by buying a ticket in a lottery. If a prize is won it may be attributed to chance and this possibility is quite sufficient to enable God's grace to function without it being so obvious as to constitute a miracle. This attitude, continues Dessler, is far-removed from that of the average believer who devotes a great part of his time and considerable intellectual and physical effort to his work or his business. On the other hand it is spiritually dangerous to rely on such a small effort as did the saint who bought the lottery ticket for if God 'tested' a man's faith by withholding His blessing he might be tempted to see his lack of effort as the reason for his failure and so be led to question God's providence. Consequently, each person is obliged to weigh carefully the amount of effort required of him so as to preserve the delicate balance between rash spiritual confidence in his power to endure the 'test' and the lack of trust which doubts whether the outcome can be left to God.[21]

Profound though this doctrine is, in its way, it suffers greatly from seeing the distinction between virtuous human endeavours and those religiously neutral in too closely defined terms. Everything is either black or white. The only activity worthy in itself is the study and practice of the *Torah*. Any other activity is no more than a necessary evil. This would not be so serious if the practice of the *Torah* were interpreted to include the pursuit of a livelihood. But this is ruled out by Dessler's definition of the value of this pursuit as no more than a 'screen' which man is duty bound to erect that he might not see the miracle. This 'screening' is the sole value of human effort, it has no intrinsic worth. No attempt is made here to bring the message of religion to bear on the works of man, no encouragement is given to the sense of vocation, there is no recognition that the search for truth of the scientist, the self-sacrifice of the medical practitioner, the skills of the artisan, the promotion of the world's work by technologists, businessmen, statesmen and administrators, clerks,

[21] *Mikhtabh Me-Elijahu*, p. 187f.

navvys and dustmen, schoolteachers, actors and housewives, can be, in themselves, part of God's purpose. (God, as William Temple said, is interested in many things besides Religion.) There is no appreciation of the spirit which inspired Ben-Gurion to defend the attitude of the *Halutzim* in Israel by saying to the Anglo-American Committee of Inquiry in 1946:

> We don't consider manual work as a curse, or as a bitter necessity, not even as a means of making a living. We consider it as a high human function, as the basis of human life, as the most dignified thing in the life of the human being, and which ought to be free, creative. Men ought to be proud of it.

You can say if you wish that the two viewpoints of Dessler and Ben-Gurion are modern re-statements of the views of R. Simeon and R. Ishmael. If so it is not at all difficult to show that in the mainstream of Jewish tradition it is the view of R. Ishmael which has prevailed.

It need hardly be said that if we leave aside all commentary and try to read the Genesis story as it stands the thought emerges clearly that work was enjoined upon man even in the Garden of Eden and that this is the meaning of 'to work it and to keep it'. It is easy to quote from the Rabbinic literature, produced by many different thinkers over a period of centuries, in support of a variety of ideas, but it must be obvious to any unbiased student of this literature that it contains numerous passages in which the value of labour as a good in itself is stressed. One such passage tells how Adam wept when he heard the sentence: 'Thou shalt eat the herb of the field'[22] because both he and his ass would eat of the same manger. But his mind was set at rest when God told him: 'In the sweat of thy brow shalt thou eat bread.'[23] Man was to be higher than the beast in working for his own livelihood.[24] One of the most popular of Rabbinic works, *The Fathers According to Rabbi Nathan*, is a com-

[22] Gen. iii, 18.
[23] Gen. iii, 19.
[24] Pes. 118a.

mentary to the section of the *Mishnah* known as *Ethics of the Fathers*. In the latter work there occurs the saying of Shemaiah (1st cent. B.C.E.): 'Love work.'[25] In *The Fathers According to Rabbi Nathan* there are a number of significant comments on this which convincingly dispel any doubts of the positive attitude of the Rabbis to human endeavour. Here it is clearly stated that Adam was obliged to work for his food even before his expulsion from the Garden of Eden.

> Rabbi Simeon ben Eleazer says: Even Adam tasted nothing before he worked, as it is said, *And He put him into the Garden of Eden to work it and to keep it;* (only then,) *Of every tree of the garden thou mayest freely eat.*[26]

In the same passage it is said:

> Rabbi Judah ben Bathyra says: If a man has no work to do, what should he do? If he has a run-down yard or run-down field let him go and occupy himself with it, for it is said, *Six days shalt thou labour and do all thy work.*[27] Now why does the verse say, *And do all thy work?* To include him who has run-down yards and fields – let him go and occupy himself with them.

Another saying recorded in the same passage runs:

> Love work: what is that? This teaches that a man should love work and that no man should hate work. For even as the *Torah* was given as a covenant, so was work given as a covenant; as it is said, *Six days* shalt thou labour, and do all thy work; but the seventh *day is a sabbath unto the Lord thy God.*[28]

It is true that the Rabbis generally considered the study of the *Torah* to be the highest pursuit of man and that where the demands of manual labour or business encroached on the preserves of *Torah* there is implicit, and sometimes explicit, condemnation, but from the above extracts and from many more statements in the Rabbinic literature it is clear that human labour is not usually considered to be no more than

[25] *'Aboth*, I, 10.
[26] Gen. ii, 15f.
[27] Ex. xx, 9.
[28] Ex. xx, 9-10. See Judah Goldin's ed. of *The Fathers According to Rabbi Nathan,* Yale University Press, 1955, Chapter 11, pp. 60-61.

a necessary evil, as Dessler would have it.[29] It is safe to say that the most representative of the Jewish teachers agree that man is a 'partner with God in the work of creation'[30] and that legitimate toil is one of the means of bringing about this co-operation between God and man.

Enough has been said to show that the ideal of *Bittahon* cannot be equated with the superficial optimism that all will be well if left to God. Human effort is essential and this effort, so far from demonstrating lack of trust, is the means by which man co-operates with God. But it is not alone the need for human co-operation which prevents us from too confidently asserting that in all circumstances God will provide. There is another factor to be considered. Religious people from the beginning of man's consciousness of God have tried to explain or to understand why God tolerates evil. In discussing this problem we are confronted with the great imponderables. No serious believer would dare to suggest that he knows the mysterious ways in which God works. His faith in the goodness of God prevents him from seeing evil as a refutation of Theism. Somehow, he is convinced, the lack of apparent meaning in the way the affairs of men are ordered is not incompatible with the existence of a benevolent Creator. What is beyond comprehension in the world of time will be understandable in the realms of eternity. But he would not claim that justice is always *immediately* vindicated and that unrighteousness *immediately* meets its deserts. He reads the cry of the Psalmist: 'I have been young and now I am old; yet have I not seen the righteous forsaken, nor his seed begging for bread'[31] as the poetic effusion of a great soul in a moment of intense faith. But he cannot help being aware, from his

[29] A useful summary of this subject is Abraham Cronbach's article in the *Universal Jewish Encyclopedia*, Vol. 6, New York, 1942, 'Labor', pp. 497-503.

[30] Sabb. 119b. A fine exposition of this idea in its relevance to modern life is to be found in A. Barth's *Dorenu Mul She'eloth Ha-Netzah*, 2nd. ed. Jer. 1955, p. 66f.

[31] Ps. xxxvii, 25.

own experience and from the religious literature of his faith, that the righteous often suffer and the wicked prosper. 'We cannot understand why the righteous suffer and the wicked prosper'[32] is sound Rabbinic teaching after all attempts at theodicy have been made. The true believer will not admit that chance operates in human affairs if by chance is meant a factor or factors outside God's control. For the believer there are no factors outside God's control. But if by chance is meant an *apparent* inconsistency, a *seeming* random element which makes nonsense of our tidy schemes then it is hard to see how the recognition of this element can be avoided. It follows that there is no guarantee that the life of integrity will necessarily be favoured with success or that the evil life will automatically result in failure or disgrace. It may be that for reasons he cannot fathom the good man is to be denied security,[33] it may be that the man who is held to be good in the eyes of the world is very far from good in the eyes of God.[34] Your true religious man could never pray:

> Although dear Lord I am a sinner,
> I have done no major crime;
> Now I'll come to Evening Service
> Whensoever I have the time.
> So, Lord, reserve for me a crown,
> And do not let my shares go down –
>
> *John Betjeman*
> (*Collected Poems*, John Murray, 1958)

[32] '*Aboth* IV, 15. Another interpretation (see Commentaries) is: 'We of this generation have neither the sufferings of the righteous nor the well-being of the wicked.' In any event this teacher recognises, as did so many of the Rabbis, that there are times when the wicked prosper and the righteous suffer.

[33] Cf. *Midrash* Gen. R. section 84 on the verse: 'And Jacob dwelt in the land of his father's sojournings. . . .' (Gen. xxxvii, 1): 'When the righteous desire to dwell in peace in this world Satan says: "It is not enough for the righteous that they are destined for eternal life, they want to live in peace in this world!" For when Jacob wanted to live in peace in this world the trouble of Joseph came upon him.'

[34] See foot of page 96.

Bittahon cannot mean, therefore, that the man of faith has confidence that God will prosper his efforts.

If God's blessing is not given without man's efforts and if, even then, there is no guarantee of success (and these two propositions, as we have seen, do not belong to a modern attempt at cruelly disembowelling faith but are implicit in the Jewish position) what does the ideal of *Bittahon* mean? It can only mean an attitude of trust of the strongest kind by which a man carries out his duties and conducts his life in the assurance that God will not allow the good to fail in any *ultimate* sense. Ultimately, the man of *Bittahon*, is convinced, the good life compensates for its hardships. The nature of this 'compensation' may be understood in terms of bliss in the Hereafter, or of growth of personality and character, or in terms of satisfaction at duty well performed, or, on the highest levels, in the delight of doing the will of God, or in all of these together. Whatever the immediate consequences of his deeds, the man of *Bittahon* believes that nothing gained by the omission of a good deed can compensate for the omission and nothing gained by the commission of an evil deed can compensate for its commission.[35] It is this assurance which produces the sense of serenity and quiet confidence said to be both the evidence and the result of complete trust in God. This assurance of *ultimate* success is far removed from the sanguine expectation of immediate successes. The man of *Bittahon* has no surety that his good deeds will yield rich dividends in terms of material prosperity, nor does he perform those deeds with that expectation in view. 'Ye shall not make with Me – gods of silver, or gods of gold. . . .'[36] is under

---

[34] Cf. Nidd. 30b that before a child is born it is made to take an oath: 'Be righteous, and be never wicked; and even if all the world tells you, "You are righteous", consider yourself wicked.'

[35] See '*Aboth* II, 1: 'Reckon the loss incurred by the fulfilment of a precept against the reward secured by its observance, and the gain gotten by a transgression against the loss it involves.'

[36] Ex. xx, 20.

stood by the *Midrash*[37] that God is not to be worshipped, as idols are worshipped, for the silver and gold He will shower on His worshippers. The man of *Bittahon* knows that he will have to pay sacrifice for much of the good he does. But his faith sustains him because it offers the assurance that the world is not the product of blind chance but the creation of a benevolent God and it frees him from the harrowing possibility that his failures, when they are not the result of personal incompetence, may be occasioned by his choice of the good. When Nebuchadnezzar orders Shadrach, Meshach, and Abed-nego to worship his golden image or be thrown into the burning fiery furnace, the three lads answer the great king:

> If our God whom we serve is able to deliver us, He will deliver us from the burning fiery furnace, and out of thy hand, O king. *But if not,* be it known unto thee, O king, that we will not serve thy gods, nor worship the golden image which thou hast set up.[38]

'*But if not*' – a prominent preacher has called this the greatest text in the Bible. Father Mapple's great sermon on the book of Jonah in Melville's *Moby Dick* makes the same point in matchless language.

> But oh! shipmates! on the starboard hand of every woe, there is a sure delight; and higher the top of that delight, than the bottom of the woe is deep. Is not the maintruck higher than the kelson is low? Delight is to him – a far, far upward and inner delight – who against the proud gods and commodores of this earth, ever stands forth his own inexorable self. Delight is to him whose strong arms yet support him, when the ship of this base treacherous world has gone down beneath him. Delight is to him, who gives no quarter in the truth, and kills, burns, and destroys all sin though he pluck it out from under the robes of Senators and Judges. Delight – top – gallant delight is to him, who acknowledges no law or lord, but the Lord his God, and is only a patriot to heaven. Delight is to him, whom all the waves of the billows of the sea of the boisterous mob can never

[37] *Mekhilta* to Ex. xx, 20, in the name of R. Akiba.
[38] Dan. iii, 17-18.

shake from this sure Keel of the Ages. And eternal delight and deliciousness will be his, who coming to lay him down, can say with his final breath – O Father! – chiefly known to me by Thy rod – mortal or immortal, here I die. I have striven to be Thine, more than to be this world's, or mine own. Yet this is nothing: I leave eternity to Thee; for what is man that he should live out the lifetime of his God?[39]

And long ago all this was said by the prophet Habakkuk:[40]

> For though the fig-tree shall not blossom,
> Neither shall fruit be in the vines;
> The labour of the olive shall fail,
> And the fields shall yield no food;
> The flock shall be cut off from the fold,
> And there shall be no herd in the stalls;
> Yet I will rejoice in the Lord,
> I will exult in the God of my salvation.

[39] *Moby Dick*, end of Chapter 9.
[40] iii, 17-18.

VII

HOLINESS

O F all the Jewish values none is so vague and indefinable, on the surface, as holiness, none that appears more remote and less relevant to life today. The holy man is thought of as an emaciated, unworldly ascetic, lost in contemplation, occasionally descending from the heights to offer guidance to lesser mortals. We have had reason to quote in previous chapters from Luzzatto's great work on the degrees of saintliness. Holiness is, in Luzzatto's text, the culmination of all the qualities he describes with deep insight. And it is clear that for Luzzatto holiness is an esoteric ideal and his holy man not far removed from the conventional picture. Luzzatto begins by stating that holiness cannot be attained by man's unaided effort. It is, in part, a divine gift, though this gift is not granted to the man who has not striven mightily to live a holy life.[1] The man who aspires to holiness must keep entirely aloof[2] from material things. He must cling[3] at all times and at all hours to that which is godly. There is no break in the communion which the soul of such a man holds with God, even when he performs those functions which his

[1] *Mesillat Yesharim*, ed. Kaplan, Philadelphia, 1936, p. 221 and the whole of Chapter 26, p. 221f.
[2] Kaplan translates this as 'keeping aloof from whatever is grossly material' but the Hebrew (*nibhdal ve-ne'etak min ha-humriyoth legamre*) is rather to be understood in the sense of 'keeping aloof entirely from material things'.
[3] The idea of *debhekuth*, 'cleaving to God,' owes much to Neo-Platonism, see Scholem *Major Trends in Jewish Mysticism*, p. 123 and notes.

physical nature demands. But man cannot attain this lofty degree without God's grace, which is finally granted to him as a reward for his perseverance. It is only when God has imparted to such a man some of His holiness that he can succeed in being in continual communion with God. Once a man has been endowed with this gift of holiness even his physical actions become holy. The physical functions are no longer a necessary evil (as they are, in Luzzatto's view, for the man who has not attained this degree) but become sacred through the personality of holy man. The very food eaten by the holy man is as an offering that has been placed on the altar, transformed through its contact with one who is in constant communion with God. None can attain even the preliminary stages of holiness (i.e. before God's special gift has been granted to him) unless he has ascended all the rungs of the ladder of saintliness described in Luzzatto's book.

> See, then, that in order to attain holiness it is necessary for a man to practice abstinence, to meditate intently upon the mysteries of Providence and the secrets of nature, and to acquire a knowledge of the majesty and attributes of God, blessed be He, so that he comes to cleave devotedly to Him and to carry out His purpose even when engaged in worldly pursuits. . . . It is impossible to attain the trait of holiness in any other way, and he who attempts to do so remains, in all respects as gross and earthly as the rest of mankind. And the things that will greatly help a man in the quest after holiness are solitude and abstinence, for when there are no distractions, the soul is able to gather strength, and to commune with the Creator.[4]

Luzzatto is insistent on the need for solitude as a prerequisite for holiness. When two people meet, he argues, the physical element in one is awakened and reinforced by the physical element in the other. But the man who courts solitude will find that with God's help his soul will become strong and he will be able to conquer all corporeal desires. The most elevated role is reserved for the holy man. His power of com-

[4] Solitude as a prerequisite for holiness is, of course, stressed by all the great mystics.

prehension will exceed mortal limitations until in his communion with God he will be entrusted with the power of
reviving the dead, as were Elijah and Elishah. He who cleaves
to God in complete self-surrender is able to derive from Him
even the power over life itself, the power which, more than
any other, is the attribute of God.[5]

There are two possible attitudes a modern man can take
with regard to Luzzatto's thesis. One is to dismiss it as evidence of something pathological in the writer's make-up and
those for whom any experience not shared by the mass of
men is labelled 'morbid' would speak here of delusions of
grandeur and psychological maladjustment. The other attitude is to appreciate that while Luzzatto's picture is bound to
be repellent and more than a little inhuman as seen with
modern eyes, this tells us nothing of the real value of holy
living. A less superficial view of the saints of the past and
their writing is to refuse to dismiss them as bizarre and
distasteful without recognising that holy men of every faith
have spoken in similar terms of the possibility of human
self-transcendence. We must acknowledge that there is much
in Luzzatto's work, and in the works of other great spiritual
masters, which corresponds to our own highest aspirations.
It is not unlikely that there may be some who, by reason of
their spiritual faculties and the zeal with which they have
obeyed them, have attained a more intense experience of the
divine than is given to most men. But however we approach
the description of holy living found in this and in kindred
works it is obvious that the ideal as here depicted is not for
us. To refuse to dismiss the most elevated descriptions of
holiness as aberrations is one thing, to pretend that we can
reach these heights is another. In any event the ideal of
holiness is, according to the Bible and much of subsequent
Jewish teaching, for all men, not alone for the hermit or the
recluse. 'And ye shall be unto Me a kingdom of priests, and

[5] *Mesillat Yesharim*, p. 228.

a holy *nation*.'⁶ 'Speak *unto all the congregation of the children of Israel,* and say unto them: Ye shall be holy; for I the Lord your God am holy."⁷ In fact, Jewish tradition appears to have made a distinction between the holy man and the man in whose life there is holiness. Only a very few of the great Jews of the past are called 'the holy'.⁸ But the ideal of holiness as a quality in one's life is held up for all Jews. Evidently this ideal is not for an esoteric group of saints but an attitude of mind and a course of action for normal men and women, living in the world and sharing in its joys and pleasures, its hopes, frustrations and ambitions. It is not easy to understand what this ideal can mean for such men and women and it is to this task that, with the sense of the provisional such a search must entail, we now address ourselves.

The root of the Hebrew word for holiness – *Kedushah* – means 'to be separate'. Reference to this root meaning is generally made by those who have tried to uncover the idea behind the term *Kedushah*. Thus the *Siphra* interprets 'Ye shall be holy'⁹ as 'Ye shall be of those who separate themselves'¹⁰ i.e. from things which contaminate spiritually. In the line of this tradition is Moses ben Nahman's (Nahmanides, 1195-c.1270) exposition of: 'Ye shall be holy."¹¹ Nahmanides commentary to the Pentateuch is one of the most profound of the mediaeval commentaries. It is printed in all the better editions of the Rabbinic Bible and still enjoys a wide popu-

---

⁶ Ex. xix, 6.
⁷ Lev. xix, 2.
⁸ E.g. Rabbi Judah the Prince, the editor of the *Mishnah*, was called *Ha-Kadosh*, 'The Holy,' it is said, because he never looked at his membrum (Sabb. 118b). Other teachers called 'The Holy' are Isaac Luria (d. 1572), the famous Saphed Kabbalist, and Isaiah Horovitz (b. c.1555 – c.1628), known as *Shelah Ha-Kadosh*, after the initial letters of his work: '*Shene Luhoth Ha-Berith.*' The martyr is generally known as *Ha-Kadosh*.
⁹ Lev. xix, 2.
¹⁰ *Siphra* to Lev. xix, 2.
¹¹ Comment. to Pentateuch on Lev. xix, 2.

larity among Jewish scholars. This author's exposition of holiness can serve as a guide to the application of the Rabbinic teachings to modern life. Nahmanides begins by quoting the *Siphra* to which we have called attention. Taking issue with *Rashi*, who understands the separation mentioned in the *Siphra* to mean separation from illicit sexual relations and other sins, Nahmanides prefers to interpret the injunction as the separation from things which are permitted. The trait of *Perishuth*,[12] 'Abstinence', is identified by Nahamides with the command to be holy.

> The principle is that the Torah forbids illicit sexual relations and forbids certain foods but it permits the sexual act in marriage and permits the eating of meat and the drinking of wine. Consequently the libertine would have found many opportunities for unlimited sexual indulgence with his wife or with his many wives, for unrestrained gluttony and drunkenness, for speaking obscene things to his heart's desire, for these things are not explicitly forbidden in the *Torah*. Such a man would be a *scoundrel with the full permission of the Torah*. Therefore, after the *Torah* had detailed those things which are categorically forbidden it enjoins man to separate himself from that which is unnecessary. . . .

Nahmanides goes on to give illustrations of this principle in two other fields, in business dealings and in the observance of the Sabbath. Though theft and fraudulent dealings are explicitly forbidden it would still be possible for a man to keep within the law and yet be a thorough scoundrel. Hence there is an explicit injunction to go beyond the letter of the law in obedience to the Higher Law of the heart.[13] Similarly, though certain types of work are explicitly forbidden on the Sabbath it would still be possible for a man to engage in many kinds of activity which, though not expressly forbidden,

---

[12] From a root meaning 'to be separate'. Some scholars understand the term *Perushim*, 'The Pharisees', to mean 'Separatists', i.e. from impurity and defilement, see Louis Finkelstein, *The Pharisees*, Vol. I, Philadelphia, 1940, p. 76.

[13] The principle of *liphnim mishurath ha-din*, 'going beyond the line of the Law' (B.K. 99a, B.M. 83a and freq.).

destroy the Sabbath atmosphere. Consequently here, too, there is a general command to rest which embraces these activities.[14]

Nahmanides follows here the Rabbinic teaching: 'Sanctify thyself with regard to that which is permitted to thee.'[15] The command to be holy is an injunction, in Nahmanides' expressive words, against being 'a scoundrel with the full permission of the *Torah*'. The point of this doctrine is that the rules and regulations of the *Torah* constitute the bare minimum of decent behaviour expected of every Jew, a standard below which none should fall. But an essential part of the *Torah* discipline is that a man is obliged to go beyond these minimum rules. For this there can be no legislation for all depends on the character and temperament of the individual. What may be morbid indulgence, leading to a softening of the moral fibre, for one, may be a necessity for another. Judaism believes in the capacity of man to decide such matters for himself. With all its insistence on rules, Judaism nevertheless acknowledges a whole area of life, the area of the licit, where man's freedom of choice must operate in determining those things which will help him to live more worthily and those which can pollute his soul. How many drinks a man should have in one evening, how much time he should spend in watching television, the kind of film and theatre performances he should see and the type of books he should read, the size of the wage-packet he gives to his employees, the limits to his patience in his family circle, the precise way in which he fulfils his charitable obligations, the stand he takes on the burning moral issues of the day, all these things cannot be matters of *Torah* legislation. But that a man's religion compels him to put these questions to himself is basic to any

[14] Nahmanides understands the verse: 'but on the seventh day thou shalt rest' (Ex. xxiii, 12) to be a general command to refrain from strenuous activity even where this does not fall under the heading of 'work'.

[15] Yeb. 20a.

sound religious outlook and it is the asking of the questions and the sincere attempt to answer them in the spirit of Judaism that is meant in the command to be holy. The capacity of knowing oneself, the desire to aim high and yet not over-reach the mark, wisdom and self-control, all are involved in making these decisions. Obedience to the Law is not an attempt to evade the responsibilities of personal decision by consulting a book for guidance whenever a significant choice has to be made. Obedience to the Law sets the pattern according to which life is to be lived. But this is a beginning, not an end. Obedience to the Law sets Jewish living apart from pagan living, but does not, in itself, transform the pagan into a Jew. This can only be done by acting on the implications of the command to be holy, a command that is among the most difficult and most challenging of *Torah* precepts.

The ideal of holiness is a constant challenge to a man and to the society to which he belongs. Its difficulty is increased by the need for drawing the line between a staunch adherence to principle and an inhuman attitude to life's problems. The holy man, in Luzzatto's sense, is 'inhuman' in that his way of life involves a shunning of normal human relationships. We have argued that for the truly holy, who choose God instead of man, the gains outweigh the losses. But ordinary men and women, for whom the ideal of holiness is intended, cannot be expected to make this terrible choice. There is a saying attributed to the first century teacher, R. Hanina ben Dosa, which goes to the heart of this problem. R. Hanina said:

> He in whom the spirit of his fellow-creatures takes delight, in him the spirit of the All-Present takes delight: and he in whom the spirit of his fellow-creatures takes not delight in him the spirit of the All-Present takes not delight.[16]

A strange evaluation on the surface, preferring, as it seems to do, popularity to integrity. As Dr. Hertz remarks, if taken

[16] *Aboth* III 10.

at its face value it does scant justice to the prophet or the martyr: human favour does not, as a rule, shadow them.[17] *Vox populi, vox Dei* has often had pernicious results when applied to life's problems.

One of the besetting faults of our age is the cult of personality glorification, ignoring the character which personality conceals. A charming manner, a pleasing exterior, courteous behaviour, and a goodly measure of the social graces – these are sufficient to veil inner depravity. The inevitable result of this stress on apparent virtue is to leave an open door through which the demagogue can enter to capture the public mind and heart.

This can hardly be the Jewish ideal. It was no doubt in opposition to the facile assumption that popularity is necessarily evidence of good character and sound leadership that a Talmudic teacher said: 'If a scholar is loved by his townsfolk it is not because he is worthy, but because he has failed to rebuke them for their religious and moral shortcomings.'[18] What then does R. Hanina mean?

The words *nohah hayemenu* in Hanina's saying are generally translated as 'takes delight in him' but a more literal translation would be 'is at ease with him'. There is no suggestion of pandering to the vulgar taste, still less of requiring the sanction of the indifferent, the ignorant, and the antagonistic before holding strong religious views. The idea conveyed here is that the course adopted in the religious life must not be of such a nature as to repel ordinary people. The way of life a man adopts, R. Hanina is saying, must be such that even those who cannot accept it for themselves can yet feel 'at ease' in its presence, can yet feel that this is a noble life.

The prophet and the martyr forfeit the love of their

[17] Comment. to the Prayer Book, Lond. 1947, p. 655.
[18] Keth. 105b, cf. the commentary of *Maharsha* who remarks that the term 'townsfolk' refers to ignorant people who are unable to assess the learning of the scholar.

fellows by stern, unrelenting insistence on obedience to the call of duty, yet they evoke feelings of profound respect even in the hearts of those who are determined to silence their voice. The message of the prophet and martyr is provocative and disturbing, but those who hear it discover an echo in their own souls. Indeed, their opposition may be an attempt to silence this echo, the struggle against it often arising out of a tacit recognition of the truth of the message. Not so the disturbance created by the fanatic, the bigot and the crank. Those who reject their ideas do so with indignation at the affront to human personality in the attempt to confuse enthusiasm for conviction and to convert a side into a main issue.

Holiness must be wedded to humanity. Martin Buber[19] has recently described how *Hasidic* values can be of relevance to modern man's predicament. One of these values, says Buber, is to be 'humanly holy'. Religious people with strong convictions are particularly prone to one-sidedness. Religious faith can be of the narrow, bitter variety which few can respect and fewer still admire. It was against this cramping conception of religious faith that R. Hanina preached. The same thought has often been voiced in subsequent Jewish teaching. It was well expressed by the *Hasidic* teacher, R. Mendel of Kotzk, who paraphrased the verse: 'Ye shall be holy *men* unto me,'[20] to mean that the ideal of holiness ought not to produce an inhuman type of person.

[19] 'Hasidism and Modern Man' in *Between East and West – Essays Dedicated to the Memory of Bela Horovitz, Lond.,* East and West Library, 1958, p. 9f.

[20] Ex. xxii, 30.

VIII

HUMILITY

MOSES, the greatest of men in the Jewish tradition, is described as the most humble: 'Now the man Moses was very meek, above all the men that were upon the face of the earth.'[1] Abraham, the father of the Jewish people, protests before his God: 'Behold now, I have taken upon me to speak unto the Lord, who am but dust and ashes.'[2] When Saul was chosen as the first king of Israel he was discovered 'hid among the baggage',[3] a phrase which has become current in Jewish speech for the man who shuns the limelight. David's retort to his wife, who despised him for so far forgetting his regal dignity that he danced before the Lord with the meanest of his people, is the eternal response of the modest man who assumes office in order to serve his people, not that they serve him: 'And I will be yet more vile than this, and will be base in mine own sight; and with the handmaids whom thou hast spoken of, with them will I get me honour.'[4] The Hebrew king was to write a copy of the Law and read therein all the days of his life, 'that his heart be not lifted up above his *brethren*'.[5] Greatness and humility, in the Hebraic tradition, are not incompatible. They complement each other. The greater the man the more humble he is expected to be and is likely to be. Because it is a principle of Rabbinic exegesis

[1] Num. xii, 3.
[2] Gen. xviii, 27.
[3] I Sam. x, 22.
[4] II Sam. vi, 22.
[5] Deut. xvii, 20.

that the attributes of God mentioned in the Bible are generally stated as a lesson to man who is to 'imitate God', the Rabbis do not hesitate to speak even of the humility of God. The third century teacher R. Johanan, remarked that wherever the greatness of God is mentioned in Scripture there His humility is mentioned, too.[6] One of the Rabbinic explanations of the strange plural form in the story of Creation: 'Let *us* make man,'[7] is that God took counsel with the angels before creating man to teach men the virtue of humility.[8] When God revealed Himself to Moses for the first time, say the Rabbis, He chose the lowly bush from which to reveal Himself.[9] The *Torah*, they say further is compared to water, for just as water runs downhill and not uphill the word of God can only be found in the heart of a humble man.[10] In the same vein, a famous mediaeval Jewish preacher noted that the prophet speaks of the earth being full of the knowledge of the Lord as the waters cover the sea.[11] Although, this teacher observed, the surface of the water of the sea is level the measure of water covering the land at the sea's bottom depends on its depth. So it is with the knowledge of the Lord. The more humble a person and the more depth to his life the greater his capacity for comprehending God's word.[12]

Greatness is married with humility because it is the great man who recognises his unworthiness in the presence of God's wisdom and might. The man who has made determined efforts to master one tiny field of human knowledge, the specialist in one little corner of wisdom, the adept in one small part of the art of living, knows something of the vast

[6] Meg. 31a.
[7] Gen. i, 26.
[8] B.R. 8, 8.
[9] B.R. 2, 5.
[10] Ta'an. 7a.
[11] Is. xi, 9.
[12] Azariah Figo, see Israel Bettan: *Studies in Jewish Preaching*, Cincinnati, 1939, p. 246.

range of possible experience and he comes to see that whatever he has achieved is as nothing to what can be achieved. But apart from this, greatness and humility are complementary, it being only the great man who avoids the many pitfalls of pride masquerading as humility. Crude vanity and self-glorification are easily recognised for what they are. Mock modesty is less easy to detect. It is not unusual for a man to take pride in his humility, nor is it unknown for a man to indulge in the more subtle form of self-deception in which he prides himself that he is not a victim of mock modesty. The famous *Hasidic* master, Israel of Ruzhyn (d. *c.*1851), was fond of quoting the verse in Jeremiah: [13] 'If a man hide himself in secret places and I, shall I not see him? saith the Lord.' With exaggerated exegetical, but shrewd psychological, insight the master of Ruzhyn interpreted the verse: 'If a man hide himself in the secret places of his heart and still say "I" then I shall not see him saith the Lord.' Luzzatto, penetratingly discussing the different forms of mock modesty writes: [14]

> Another imagines that he is so great and so deserving of honour that no one can deprive him of the usual signs of respect. And to prove this, he behaves as though he were humble and goes to extremes in displaying boundless modesty and infinite humility. But in his heart he is proud, saying to himself, 'I am so exalted, and so deserving of honour, that I need not have any one do me honour. I can well afford to forgo marks of respect.' Another is the coxcomb, who wants to be noted for his superior qualities and to be singled out for his behaviour. He is not satisfied with having every one praise him for the superior traits which he thinks he possesses, but he wants them also to include in their praises that he is the most humble of men. He thus takes pride in his humility, and wishes to be honoured because he pretends to flee from honour. Such a prig usually goes so far as to put himself below those who are much inferior to him, even below the meanest, thinking that in this way he displays the utmost humility. He refuses all titles of greatness and declines promotion in rank, but in his heart he thinks, 'There is no one

[13] Jer. xxiii, 24.
[14] *Mesillat Yesharim*, ed. M. M. Kaplan, p. 104f.

in all the world as wise and as humble as I.' Conceited people of this type, though they pretend mightily to be humble, cannot escape some mishap which causes their pride to burst forth, like a flame out of a heap of litter. . . . Finally, there are the proud who manage so to conceal their pride that it does not express itself in their conduct. Men of this type consider themselves great sages, and think they know the truth about everything. They consider very few their equals in wisdom, and disregard what others have to say. They imagine that whatever they find difficult to understand cannot possibly be intelligible to any one else. . . .

The Jews of Eastern Europe used to tell of a man who came to his Rabbi with a complaint. 'All my life I have tried to follow the advice of the Rabbis that he who runs away from honour, honour will pursue him,[15] and yet honour has not pursued me.' 'The trouble,' the Rabbi replied, 'is that you keep looking over your shoulder to see if honour is really pursuing you!' Hence the connection between greatness and humility. The great man is capable of knowing himself to some extent, of arriving at a more or less objective estimate of his true worth without yielding to the temptations of either exaggerated self-esteem or false self-depreciation. The paradox here is that when a man knows his worth he is liable to be a victim of pride but when he consciously tries to overlook his own achievements and abilities the trap of self-delusion yawns in his path. And though, as we have seen, Jewish teaching tends to suggest that the greater the man the less attraction pride will have for him a reading of human history shows only too clearly that not many are great in this sense. 'The last infirmity of great minds' is not easily conquered.

How escape the dilemma? One of the wisest teachings on the attainment of humility is a letter of advice written by Nahmanides (1195-c.1270) to his son:[16]

[15] 'Erub. 13b.
[16] Israel Abrahams: *Hebrew Ethical Wills*, Phil., 1948, p. 94f., B. Halper's *Post Biblical Literature*, Phil., 1943, p. 171f. The translation used here is that of Abrahams.

Accordingly I will explain how thou must habituate thyself to the quality of humility in thy daily practice. Let thy voice be low, and thy head bowed; let thine eyes be turned earthwards and thy heart heavenwards. Gaze not in the face of him whom thou dost address. Every man should seem in thine eyes as one greater than thyself. If he be wise or wealthy, it is thy duty to show him respect. If he be poor and thou the richer, or if thou be wiser than he, bethink thee in thy heart, that thou art the more guilty, he is the more innocent. If he sin, it is from error; if thou sin, it is with design!

Nahmanides advises his son to consider all men his superiors. For if they are really superior to him in wisdom or achievements there is no call for pride. But even in comparison with those obviously inferior he has no cause for self-congratulation for it may well be that precisely because of their disabilities their responsibilities are the less and, for all he knows to the contrary, they may be fulfilling their obligations with greater success than he has attained in fulfilling his. Humility, in this view, consists in the recognition that God alone knows the true worth of a man and the extent to which he faces life's challenge with the gifts, or lack of them, that are his portion. The religious basis for humility lies in the appreciation that only God can know the true worth of a man. The *Besht* interpreted the verse: 'And we know not how we serve the Lord, until we come hither'[17] to mean that no one can know if he has really served God until he arrives in the world of truth after death. The Rabbis long before the *Besht* told of the great R. Johanan ben Zakkai weeping on his death bed because of his uncertainty as to how he would fare in the Hereafter.[18] It was no doubt a similar thought of the great-grandson of the *Besht*, Nahman of Bratzlav (1772-1811), when he taught that the antidote to pride is faith, basing his idea on the verse: 'When thy faithfulness is round about thee thou rulest the proud'![19]

[17] Ex. x, 26.
[18] Ber. 28b.
[19] Ps. lxxxix, 9-10.

HUMILITY

On the deeper level humility consists not so much in thinking little of oneself as in not thinking of oneself at all. The quality is one of self-forgetfulness rather than of self-denigration. When the mystics, in particular, dwell on the virtues of self-forgetfulness, or, to use the far stronger term popular with the *Habad* sect of the *Hasidim*, 'self-abnegation',[20] they are not thinking of a conscious effort of the will. To try to nullify the self by calling attention to it, ends in failure. The way to this kind of humility is rather to become

---

[20] *Bittul Ha-Yesh.* This doctrine is found in earlier sources but is particularly bound up with *Habad* ideas on the illusionary nature of this world. Reminiscent of Hindu ideas, the *Habad* doctrine teaches that in 'reality' only God exists. Shneor Zalman of Ladi (1747-1812), the founder of the *Habad* school, expounds in a highly original way, the Kabbalistic idea that God 'withdrew from Himself into Himself' (*Tzimtzum*) in order to leave room for the world. According to Shneor Zalman, this withdrawal does not really take place in God but only appears to do so. From the point of view of His creatures the world and God are separate but from God's point of view, as it were, there is no finite world at all. 'Know this day, and lay it to thy heart, that the Lord, He is God in heaven above and upon the earth beneath; *there is none else*' (Deut. iv, 39) is understood by Shneor Zalman to mean quite literally that there is nothing apart from God (*Tanya, Sha'ar Ha-Yihud Ve-Ha-Emunah*, Chapters I-XII). For classical theists, such as the Gaon of Vilna, this was heretical doctrine and is frequently mentioned as one of the chief counts against Hasidim in the polemical literature of the period. But this doctrine is not to be confused with Spinoza's pantheism. For pantheism God and the Universe are one, the transcendent aspect of the Deity is ignored or rejected; for the *Habad* thinkers God contains the Universe but transcends it. In fact, in the *Habad* view, there is no Universe (for a full exposition of *Habad* theories the best work is still M. Teitelbaum's *Ha-Rav Mi-Ladi*, Vol. II, pp. 37-94). The lengthy discussion of panentheism in *Philosophers Speak of God* by Charles Hartshorne and William L. Reese, University of Chicago Press, 1953, is relevant to the *Habad* view, see particularly the remarks on pp. 163-164. Dubnow and others have tried to identify the *Habad* view with that of Shneor Zalman's near-contemporary, Bishop Berkeley, in whose idealistic philosophy the

Universe is an idea in the Mind of God. But the two theories are
actually poles apart. There are two well-known limericks on
Berkeley's view:

> There was a young man who said, 'God
> Must find it exceedingly odd
> If the sycamore tree
> Continues to be
> When there's no one about in the Quad.'

REPLY

> Dear Sir:
> Your astonishment's odd:
> *I'm* always about in the Quad.
> And that's why the tree
> Will continue to be,
> Since observed by
> *Yours faithfully,*
> God.

For Berkeley the tree 'continues to be' because it is present in
the Mind of God. For Shneor Zalman the tree is, in fact, non-
existent, as is the Quad, and for that matter, the young man!
As a direct result of this idea, humility in *Habad* thought means
the recognition that All is in God, hence the doctrine of self-
abnegation, *Bittul Ha-Yesh*. It is said that Shneor Zalman once
asked a disciple: 'What do we mean when we say "God"?' 'I, too,
do not know,' said the Rabbi, 'but I must say it, for it is so, and
therefore I must say it: He is definitely there, and except for
him nothing is definitely there – and this is He' (Buber: *Tales
of the Hasidim*, Vol. I, New York, 1947, p. 269). Similar ideas
have been held, of course, by the mystics of every age. See, for
example, Aldous Huxley's quotation from Fenelon on how to attain
humility (*The Perennial Philosophy*, Chatto & Windus): 'Two
things combined will bring that about; you must never separate
them. The first is contemplation of the deep gulf, whence God's
all-powerful hand has drawn you out, and over which He ever
holds you, so to say, suspended. The second is the presence of
that all-penetrating God. It is only in beholding and loving God
that we can learn forgetfulness of self, measure duly the nothing-
ness which has dazzled us, and accustom ourselves thankfully
to decrease beneath that great Majesty which absorbs all things.
Love God and you will be humble; love God and you will throw
off the love of self; love God and you will love all that He gives
you to love for love of Him.'

absorbed in worthy aims for their own sake. The value of self-renunciation, the expansiveness, the enlargement of soul it produces have been attested to by the most diverse thinkers from Buddha and Lao-Tze to Shaw. There is certainly evidence that some of the greatest Jews approached life in this way. Reading the prophetic books, for instance, one is struck by the way in which the *message* counts for everything, its bearer for very little. Professor Louis Finkelstein has recently commented on the remarkable phenomenon of anonymity of utterance in the Bible and in subsequent Jewish writings. The ancients appear to have had none of the modern's desire to acquire immortality through his work. It was the word of God that was to live on, not the man who conveyed it. The *Habad* teachers were fond of quoting the verse: 'And there was not a man to till the ground.'[21] He who is 'not a man', who has transcended the self, he can make the earth yield all its treasures.

The modern virtue of self-respect is not necessarily at variance with true humility. The humble man need not be lacking in aplomb and self-possession.[22] True, certain forms of exaggerated self-assertiveness are no more than attempts at compensation for feelings of inferiority. But here the teachings

---

[21] Gen. ii, 5.

[22] It is worthy of note in this connection that Maimonides in his 'Eight Chapters' (ed. Joseph I. Gorfinkle, Columbia University Press, 1912, Chapter IV, pp. 55-6), following the Aristotelian doctrine of the divine Mean, advises the adoption of the mean between arrogance and self-abasement and considers this to be true humility. However, in his Commentary to *'Aboth*, IV, 4 and in the *Yad, Hil. De'oth*, II, 3, Maimonides advises that in the matter of humility the extreme is to be followed, not the mean: 'There are, however, some dispositions in regard to which it is wrong to pursue even a middle course, but the contrary extreme is to be embraced, as, for instance, in respect to pride. One does not follow the proper path by merely being humble. Man should be very humble and extremely meek.' Cf. Gorfinkle's note 2 on page 60-62.

of the mystics are to the point that in the attainment of humility the intellect should be encouraged to forget all considerations of both inferiority and superiority. That such a state of mind is difficult, if not impossible, for most men does not detract from the ideal, though one, perhaps, never fully to be realised. As in other fields, Judaism does not overlook the tensions which exist between the ideal and reality and it does not abandon the ideal even though it makes no attempt to demand the impossible. Every religious faith must teach that 'a man's reach must exceed his grasp or what's a heaven for?' On the other hand, the Rabbis remind us that 'the *Torah* was not given to the ministering angels'.[23] This is Judaism's strength that there is no limit to the lofty flights of soul of which its saints have been capable, and yet its minimum requirements are such as to be well within the reach of ordinary men and women. Humility is among the highest of the Jewish virtues and in its highest formulations capable of realisation only by the most intrepid.[24] But in some form it is expected of every Jew; it belongs to the 'inheritance of the children of Jacob'. And rightly understood and followed the ideal of humility has no corroding effects on man's character and personality but is itself not alone the fruit of greatness but a powerful spur to greatness. The *Torah*, say the Rabbis, was given on the lowliest of the mountains.[25] True, but it was given on a mountain. To remain in the safety and ease of the valley when mountains are to be climbed, is neither greatness nor humility. To climb the mountain and

---

[23] Yom. 30a, Kidd. 54a, originally applied to the impossibility of humans to take excessive care with regard to physical purity but later applied in the literature of Jewish piety to convey the idea that too much cannot be expected from man with his physical limitations.

[24] In Luzzatto's ladder of virtue, which follows Rabbinic teaching, humility occupies the third highest rung, being considered superior even to saintliness, ed. Kaplan, p. 192f.

[25] Sot. 5a.

then survey those down in the valley with cold contempt, is neither humility, nor true greatness. To climb the mountain and yet gaze on the peaks still unconquered, this is greatness and humility.

IX

THE LOVE OF NEIGHBOUR

Love thy neighbour as thyself"[1] is the golden rule of Judaism as it is of other faiths. All the higher religions agree with the philosophers, whose concern was with ethics rather than religion, that the love of one's fellows is an integral part of the good life. It is not very helpful to debate who thought of the rule first. Jews need not make the sorry attempt at bolstering up their faith by claiming that this teaching is original with Judaism nor need they have any cause for alarm if it can be shown that others had conceived of this tremendous idea before it was recorded in the Bible. Such a rule is the natural consequence of human striving for the good life. Religious people will say that it is evidence of the divine spark in man that this and other basic truths can be arrived at by the human mind and through the human heart even without the aid of revelation. As has been said, 'a thing is not true because it is in the *Torah*, it is in the *Torah* because it is true.'

The original rule in Hebrew consists of three words – *ve-'ahabhta* ('And thou shalt love'), *le-re'akha* ('thy neighbour'), *kamokha* ('as thyself'). If we are to understand Jewish teaching on this subject it is necessary to examine each of these words in detail with a view to uncovering its implications.

Ve-'ahabhta–'And thou shalt love'–is generally interpreted as a *command* to love. The Codifiers give it as one of the positive precepts of the *Torah*. In many of the older Prayer Books there is a rubric which refers to the teaching of

[1] Lev. xix, 18.

the great Kabbalist, Isaac Luria (d. 1572), that before his prayers a man should resolve to keep the *precept* of loving his neighbour. The formula for this resolution is given as: 'Behold I accept the positive command of "Thou shalt love thy neighbour as thyself." ' In a previous chapter we have considered the difficulties inherent in the command to love God. Some of these apply with equal force here. The emotions cannot be turned on like a tap. If a man loves his neighbour no command is necessary. If he has no love for his neighbour no command will be effective. Bahya's famous classic, dealing with such precepts as 'Love thy neighbour', is called *The Duties of the Heart*. But this is precisely the difficulty – how can there be *duties* of the heart?

Jewish tradition has two answers to this question: one, if it may be put in this way, on the lower level of religious experience, the other on a higher level. The first answer would be that the golden rule is not, in fact, an appeal to the emotions but a call to action. It is frequently overlooked that the full text of the verse containing the golden rule runs: 'Thou shalt not take any vengeance, nor bear any grudge against the children of thy people, but thou shalt love thy neighbour as thyself: I am the Lord.'[2] This is to say that the golden rule can be paraphrased: 'Love thy neighbour as thyself by not doing to him that which you would not have him do to you. Therefore, do not take revenge or bear any grudge against him.' It is well known that the great Hillel gave this kind of paraphrase to the Gentile who asked to be taught the whole of the *Torah* in one maxim.[3] Seen in this light the emphasis is on the *deed* and this can be commanded.

But this is no more than the minimum requirement of the Jewish ethic, the standard at which every Jew is expected to aim. But Jewish teaching knows, too, of the higher sense in which the golden rule is an appeal to the heart, of the more severe demands made on those who would seek to tread the

[2] Lev. xix, 18.
[3] Sabb. 31a.

difficult road of self-improvement. And in reply to the question how can love be commanded? it would say that the command is for love so to be cultivated that it becomes second-nature. The paradox here, as a prominent Jewish moralist has said, is that the precept of loving the neighbour is not fulfilled until one is not aware that a precept is being fulfilled. The love of the neighbour is to become a spontaneous reaction. To be consciously aware that one is carrying out a religious duty – a *mitzvah* – is to sacrifice the essence of the *mitzvah*.

How can this love be cultivated? One of the ways is by constant obedience to the golden rule in the first sense we have noted. Judaism believes in the healing effect of action. By doing things in obedience to lofty ideals we bring down those ideals from Heaven. They become nearer, more real; we make them our own. By refraining from doing harm to others, by practising charity and benevolence, we gradually learn to express our personalities in this way and our character changes for the better. Judaism does not accept the view that human nature cannot be changed.

Another method is to reflect deeply on the Jewish teachings concerning God and man. A distinction has been made, with justice, between *loving* and *liking*. When a girl refuses a proposal of marriage by saying: 'I am very sorry, I am fond of you but I do not love you' she is not using the word *love* in the sense in which it is used in the golden rule. Obviously, the particular attraction that is the basis of married love, or the special regard of members of a family for each other, cannot be extended to embrace other people. ('As thyself,' for that matter, cannot be understood in this way for we do not love ourselves in the same way as we love those dear to us, where the essence of that love is a giving of the self.) There are, too, people whom we positively dislike and others we have never met. We cannot positively *like* such people but we can *love* them. For the word *ve-'ahabhta* refers to the sympathy, understanding and the desire for identification

with other human beings which results from reflection on our
common humanity, that all human beings have the same
basic needs, are hurt in the same way and pleased in the same
way, that their happiness is our happiness and their misery
our misery. Rabbi Moses Cordovero (1522-1570) the great
Safed mystic said that all men's souls are united with each
other because they all stem from Adam's soul so that to love
one's neighbour is to love oneself! [4] Judaism teaches that all
men are created in God's image, that He loves us all and has
a place for each in His purpose. It is no coincidence that the
verse containing the golden rule concludes with the words:
'I am the Lord.' Much has been said on the relation between
religion and ethics. It is obviously untrue to suggest that there
can be no ethics without religion, that non-religious people
cannot be good in the ethical sense. But religion elevates
ethics on to a totally different plane. From the religious view-
point the ethical life is far more than a system evolved by
society for its survival. It is far more than a 'social contract' in
which *A* agrees not to harm *B* in return for *B*'s assurance that
he will not harm *A*. The ethical life is a religious imperative
because God who gave us life gave it to our fellows, because
if it can be said that God needs *any* man He needs *every* man.
It was in this spirit that a *Hasidic* master said: 'Would that
I loved the greatest saint as much as God loves the greatest
sinner.'

The second Hebrew word in the golden rule – *le-re'akha*,
'thy neighbour,' also requires elucidation. Is a fellow-Israelite
meant? Or does the rule embrace all men? Dr. Hertz, in
attempting to refute the view that the morality of the golden
rule is tribal writes: [5]

[4] *Tomer Debhorah*, ed. Z. W. Aschkenazi, Jer. 1928, Chapter I, p. 5.
Cf. the Commentary of *Malbim* to Lev. xix, 18. *Malbim* rightly
observes that affection is spoken of in Scripture as 'loving like
his own soul' e.g. in I Sam. xviii, 1 and xx, 17 and that this kind
of love cannot be extended to all men and is not meant in the
Golden Rule.

[5] In *The Pentateuch and Haftorahs*, Lond., 1938, pp. 563-564.

One need not be a Hebrew scholar to convince oneself of the fact that *re'a* means neighbour of whatever race or creed. Thus in Exodus xi, 2 – 'Let them ask every man of his neighbour and every woman of her neighbour, jewels of silver, etc.' – the Hebrew word for *neighbour* cannot possibly mean 'fellow-Israelite', but distinctly refers to the Egyptians. As in all the moral precepts of Scripture, the word *neighbour* in Lev. xix, 18, is equivalent to 'fellow man', and it includes in its range every human being by virtue of his humanity. In order to prevent any possible misunderstanding, the command of love of neighbour is in *v.* 34 of this same nineteenth chapter of Leviticus extended to include the homeless alien. 'The stranger (*ger*) that sojourneth with you shall be unto you as the homeborn among you, and thou shalt love him as thyself; for ye were strangers (*gerim*) in the land of Egypt.'*

Dr. Hertz's apology is ingenuous. It is hard to believe that if *re'a* embraced all men Scripture should find it necessary to refer to the stranger 'in order to prevent any possible misunderstanding'. Certainly the word *re'a* in Exodus refers to the Egyptians but this is because the word simply means 'neighbour'. The neighbours from whom the Israelites were to borrow the jewels of silver were Egyptians. But it would appear from the context in Leviticus that the word is used of an Israelite neighbour.

The truth of the matter is surely this: that the society for which the nineteenth chapter of the book of Leviticus legislates is one in which there are no non-Israelites, with the exception of the *ger* (stranger) who has come from another land to settle in the land of Israel. Though the term *re'a* refers to an Israelite this is not because of any intention to exclude the non-Israelite but simply because the society spoken of is one in which there are no non-Israelites. But in a different society where Israelites lived together with non-Israelites the implications of the general rule would be extended to include the latter. (Similarly, in English law the term 'person' generally refers to one residing in England and

* Hertz, in the same passage has an interesting excursus on the positive and negative forms of the Golden Rule.

hence governed by English law. Obviously no conclusions can be drawn from this that English law does not consider the members of other nationalities as 'persons'.) That this is so can be seen from the universalistic teachings of the great Hebrew prophets and the lesson of God's tender compassion for the non-Israelite sinners of Nineveh emphasised by the book of Jonah as well as from the mainfold universalistic teachings of the Rabbis.[7] One cannot pretend that in the vast range of Jewish literature there are no particularistic, exclusive views, especially those aroused by harsh discriminations against Jews, but it can safely be said that the highest and most typical teaching of Judaism is universalistic and all-embracing.[8]

We turn now to the third word of the golden rule – *kamokha*, 'as thyself'. Can one love another as much as oneself? This question is partly answered by the two interpretations we have mentioned of the command to love. According to the first interpretation the words 'as thyself' mean that a man must refrain from harming others just as he naturally refrains from harming himself. According to the second interpretation 'as thyself' means that the regard a man has for his own well-being should be extended to all men. 'As thyself' does not refer to the *degree* of concern for others but to its existence. It is as if Scripture said, let not thy thoughts, feelings and emotions be centred on thyself. Luzzatto again is of help here. He describes the arguments of the *Yetzer*, the evil inclination, in man:

'If you want to grant that man the favour which he refused to you when in need, you do not have to grant it to him cheerfully.

[7] See particularly Joseph Bloch's *Israel and the Nations*, Vienna, 1927 and Montefiore and Loewe's *A Rabbinic Anthology*, London, 1938.

[8] Relevant to this matter is S. Schechter's chapter on the election of Israel in *Some Aspects of Rabbinic Theology*, Lond., 1909, p. 57f. Cf. Louis Ginzberg's lengthy note in his *Legends of the Jews*, Vol. V, Philadelphia, 1942, p. 8, note 8.

You may refuse to retaliate, but you do not have to be his benefactor or to offer him help. If you insist upon extending considerable help to him, do so at least without his knowledge. It is not necessary for you to associate with him and again become his friend. If you have forgiven him, it is enough that you do not show yourself to him as his enemy; if you are willing to go further and associate with him once more, at least do not display as much love as formerly.' With these and similar sophistries, the evil *Yetzer* endeavours to seduce men's hearts. The *Torah* therefore lays down a general rule which takes all these possibilities into account. 'Thou shalt love thy neighbour as thyself', as thyself, without difference or distinction, without subterfuge and mental reservation, literally as thyself.[9]

Martin Buber has given a fine turn to the words 'as thyself', suggesting the words to mean: look upon thy neighbour as a *person*, not as a *thing*. Remember that he, too, exists in his own right as God's image and not merely as a means of enabling you to use him for your ends, not even for the exercise of your benevolent instincts. As you are a person so he, too, is a person.

Here is the place to consider the Jewish point of view with regard to self-sacrifice. 'Greater love hath no man than this, that a man lay down his life for his friends.'[10] This teaching has long been considered as part of the ripest fruits of Christianity. It is believed that in a man's capacity for self-sacrifice in the interests of others, the finest flowering of Christian character is seen. What is the attitude of Judaism to the question of giving one's life that another may live? Would the act of a Sydney Carton in *A Tale of Two Cities* be allowed, or even advocated, by Jewish teaching, or would it be condemned?

Jewish teachers in modern times have been nearly unanimous in their rejection of this doctrine in the name of Jewish ethic. But one entertains the suspicion that their repudiation is not so much the result of a careful examination of the

[9] *Mesillat Yesharim*, ed. Kaplan, p. 93.
[10] John xv, 13.

classic sources, as the desire to defend at all costs the *ethical* distinctions between Judaism and Christianity in an age when the doctrinal and theological differences between the two faiths are treated as irrelevant or 'remote'. *Ahad Ha-Am,* for instance, remarks in his polemic against Claude Montefiore's espousal of some aspects of the Christian ethic to the detriment of the Jewish,[11] that while Christianity is based on the concept of love, Judaism is based on that of justice. Love demands that a man give his life for his friend; justice that life is not his own to give. Love advocates the most excessive altruism; justice, that altruism is an inverted form of egotism. *Ahad Ha-Am* states that the difference between Jewish morality and that of the Gospels is not merely one of degree, but is of the very basis of morality. The Christian ethic is 'subjective'; the Jewish ethic 'objective', based on absolute justice, attaching moral value to the individual as such, without any distinction between the 'self' and the 'other'.

> All men, including the self, are under obligation to develop their lives and their faculties to the limit of their capacity and, at the same time, each is under obligation to assist his neighbour's self-development, as far as he can. But just as I have no right to ruin another man's life for the sake of my own, so I have no right to ruin my own life for the sake of another's. Both of us are men, and both our lives have the same value before the throne of justice.

Ahad Ha-Am quotes in support of this highly debatable thesis, the well-known passage in the earliest Halakhic Midrash, the *Siphra*:[12] 'If two men are travelling on a journey[13] and one of them has a pitcher of water, if both drink they will both die, but if only one drinks he will reach civilisation. Ben Petura taught that it is better that both

[11] *Essays, Letters, Memoirs – Ahad Ha-Am,* translated by Leon Simon, East and West Library, Oxford, 1946, p. 128f.

[12] *Siphra,* ed. Weiss, *Behar* VI, p. 109c, B.M. 62a.

[13] The *Siphra* has the reading 'in the desert' but in B.M. the reading is 'on the way', cf. Bacher: *Die Agada der Tannaiten,* Pt. I, Chapter 4, 6.

should drink and die, rather than that one of them should behold his companion's death. Until Rabbi Akiba came and taught: "that thy brother may live *with* thee",[14] thy life takes precedence over his life.' 'Little is known,' concludes *Ahad Ha-Am,* 'of Ben Petura and his view is certainly not adopted.'[15] Akiba's voice is that of authentic Judaism.

Dr. J. H. Hertz follows *Ahad Ha-Am.* Writing in his *Commentary to the Pentateuch* on the Golden Rule in Judaism, he remarks:

> Rabbi Akiba could not agree that two should perish where death demands but one as its toll. And, indeed, if the *Torah* had meant that a man must love his neighbour to the extent of sacrificing his life for him, in all circumstances, it would have said 'Thou shalt love thy neighbour *more than thyself.*' There are those, both in ancient and modern times, who do not agree with Rabbi Akiba, and who deem the view of Ben Petura the more altruistic, the more heroic. Such would have preferred that the words *as thyself* had not occurred in the Golden Rule. Others again preach the total annihilation of self, or at any rate, its total submergence as the basic principle of human conduct. New formulations of the whole duty of man have in consequence been proposed by various thinkers. We need examine but one of these formulations – *Live for others.* Were such a rule translated into practice, it would lead to absurdity. For *Live for others* necessarily entails that others live for you. You are to attend to everybody else's concerns, and everybody else is to attend to your concerns – except yourself. A moment's examination of this or any other proposed substitute for 'Thou shalt love thy neighbour as thyself' only brings out more clearly the fundamental sanity of Judaism.

Now while Dr. Hertz is undoubtedly correct that it would be an absurdity to expect *all* men to love others more than themselves, his denial that Judaism would expect this of *any* man is open to question. The Rabbis do speak frequently of the loftier standards demanded of the saint, of the *mishnath*

[14] Lev. xxv, 36.

[15] Lauterbach, *Rabbinic Essays,* Hebrew Union College Publications, Cincinnati, Ohio, 1951, p. 539, roundly disposes of the view that Ben Petura is Jesus.

hasidim. It is hoped that the following observations will help to refute so pedestrian a view of the Jewish ethic as that of *Ahad Ha-Am* and Dr. Hertz. Sanity and balance are wholly admirable, but is it true that Judaism has no use for the 'fool of God'?

While our problem is not dealt with explicitly in the Bible, there are a number of relevant Scriptural passages. That many of the Biblical characters risk their lives in war for the sake of their people, and are commended for so doing, has no real bearing on our question for they were fighting for themselves as well as for others. More to the point is Deborah's praise of Zebulun and Naphtali, who 'jeoparded their lives unto the death in the high places of the field',[16] i.e., they bore the brunt of Sisera's attack, unlike some of the other tribes who thought only of themselves.[17] Abraham, too, risks his life in order to save his kinsman Lot:

> And when Abraham heard that his brother was taken captive, he armed his trained servants, born in his own house, three hundred and eighteen, and pursued them unto Dan. . . . And he brought back all the goods, and also brought again his brother Lot, and his goods, and the women also, and the people.[18]

Later, Lot, too, risks his life giving shelter to the angels.[19] On the other hand, both Abraham and Isaac adopt the subterfuge of pretending that their wife is their sister, in order to protect themselves,[20] but there is no suggestion that Scripture condones their behaviour. If anything, the narratives voice an implicit condemnation of it. The Rabbis were close to the spirit of the Tamar narrative when they said[21] that Tamar was prepared to allow herself to be burnt rather than put Judah to shame.[22] Moses risks his life by smiting the

[16] Judges v, 18.
[17] See Judges v, 15-17 and 23.
[18] Gen. xiv, 14-16.
[19] Gen. xix.
[20] Gen. xii, 10-20; xx, 1-18; xxvi, 6-11.
[21] Sot. 10b.
[22] See Gen. xxxviii, 25.

Egyptian[23] and by delivering the daughters of Jethro from the shepherds.[24] When his people sinned, Moses offers his life in his prayer of intercession: 'Yet if thou wilt forgive their sin; – and if not, blot me, I pray thee, out of thy book which thou hast written.'[25] And when God wants to exterminate the people, and make of Moses 'a greater and mightier nation', he refuses to allow it.[26] Samson kills himself in order to slay the Philistines, the enemies of his people.[27] David places his life in jeopardy when he accepts the challenge of Goliath.[28] In all these passages, there is implicit the thought that it is a natural thing for men, at times, to consider others even at the risk of their own safety. Indeed, the Gospels do not suggest that Jesus was advancing any new doctrine when he said: 'Greater love hath no man than this.' He mentions it to his disciples as axiomatic, as the established view of his day. If this is correct, not only was the doctrine of 'Greater love . . .' part of the general Jewish attitude, but was recognised as such by the Gospel writers, who lay no claim to originality in this teaching.

To turn to the teachings of the *Halakhah,* we must first consider the general Halakhic attitude to self-sacrifice for the sake of a good cause. The verse: 'Which if a man do he shall *live* in them'[29] is quoted[30] in support of the unanimously accepted Rabbinic teaching that it is permitted to transgress a *Torah* precept in order to save one's life. There are, however, certain exceptions to this rule. The Jew is expected to give his life rather than worship idols, commit adultery or incest, or murder.[31] Later teachers decided that in times of

[23] Ex. ii, 11-15.
[24] Ex. ii, 17-19.
[25] Ex. xxxii, 32.
[26] Num. xiv, 2-20.
[27] Judges xvi, 28-30.
[28] I Sam. xvii.
[29] Lev. xviii, 5.
[30] Yom. 85b and freq.
[31] Sanh. 74a.

religious persecution by the ruling power, a Jew must incur martyrdom rather than transgress even a minor precept.[32] The history of Jewish martyrdom affords sufficient evidence that these teachings were followed in practice. According to Maimonides,[33] where there is no obligation for a Jew to give his life for the *Torah*, he is guilty of committing suicide if he allows himself to be killed. But other authorities rule that, while there is no obligation, it is an act of piety to give one's life,[34] if a Gentile compels a Jew to offend against his religion by transgressing *any* of the precepts of the *Torah*.[35] According to some commentators, Maimonides would concur in this if the man concerned was a renowned saint, determined to provide an object lesson for his people.[36]

There is a rather curious tale in the Talmud of a man who conceived a violent passion for a certain woman so that his life was endangered. The doctors, who were consulted, said that he could only be cured if she submitted to him but the Sages ruled: 'Let him die rather than that she should yield.' Then the doctors said: 'Let her stand nude before him' but the Sages answered: 'Sooner let him die.' Then the doctors said: 'Let her converse with him from behind a fence.' 'Let him die,' replied the Sages, 'rather than she should converse with him from behind a fence.'[37] Two opinions are then recorded.[38] Some say that the woman in the case was a married woman and this would then be an extension of the rule that adultery may not be committed even to save life. But others say that she was an unmarried woman and yet the case was treated in so severe a fashion either because of 'the disgrace to her family' or 'that the daughters of Israel may not be immorally dissolute.'

[32] Sanh. loc. cit.
[33] *Yad, Hil. Yesode Ha-Torah*, V. 1 and 4.
[34] Tos. A.Z. 27b, s.v. *yakhol.*
[35] See *Yoreh De'ah*, 157, 1.
[36] *Keseph Mishneh* to *Yad* loc. cit.
[37] Sanh. 75a.
[38] Sanh. ibid.

It follows, from the above-mentioned rule, that whatever are the views of the Rabbis on sacrificing one's life to save another's, they agree in condemning the sacrifice of another's life to save one's own. The Talmud tells of a man who came before Raba (299-352 C.E.) and said to him: 'The governor of my town has ordered me: "Go and kill so-and-so; and if not I will kill you." ' Raba replied: 'Let him kill you rather than that you should commit murder; what reason do you see for thinking that your blood is redder? Perhaps his blood is redder.'[39] As Rashi explains,[40] although it is permissible to sin in order to save one's life, this cannot apply to the crime of murder. For here, either way, a life is lost so that the commission of the crime does not save a life. From the moral point of view, the only reason there can be for preferring one's own life is that it is of greater value. But no human being can know which life is of greater value.[41] Hence, it is forbidden to save one's life by committing murder. The Talmud adduces no Scriptural proof for this, considering it to be self-evident – it is a *sabara,* 'common sense'. It would seem, moreover, from Raba's ruling that even a great scholar and saint would be prohibited from saving his life at the expense of the meanest member of the community, for here, too, it could be argued that, for all we know to the contrary, the life of the latter would be the worthier in God's eyes. In a fascinating Responsum on this question, Rav Kook even suggests that a number of men would be prohibited from saving their lives, at the expense of one man, for in the eyes of God that one man may count more than all the others.[42]

---

[39] Pes. 25b.

[40] Pes. ad loc.

[41] This *motif* appears in the well-known Talmudic anecdote (Pes. 50a) of the Rabbi who was transported to the next world, where he observed a 'topsy-turvey world', the insignificant on earth of great significance there, and the significant on earth, of no significance there.

[42] *Mishpat Kohen,* Jer. 1937, No. 143

THE LOVE OF NEIGHBOUR

Talmudic literature deals not alone with the question of committing murder in order to save one's life, but with the more complicated question of handing a man over to be murdered in order to save one's life. The *Mishnah*[43] states concerning a parallel case:

> If Gentiles said to many women: 'Give us one from among you that we may defile her, and if not, we will defile you all,' let them defile all, but let them not betray to them one soul of Israel.

Solomon Ibn Adret (1235-1310) rules that even if one of the women was of bad repute (as in Maupassant's famous tale), the others are forbidden to save their virtue by giving her to the Gentiles.[44] The Jerusalem Talmud[45] to this section of the *Mishnah* adds:

> It was taught: If a company of men travelling on a journey were held up by Gentiles, who said to them: 'Give us one of you and we will kill him, and if not we will kill all of you,' let them all be killed and let them not betray to them one soul of Israel. But if the Gentiles specified one of the company, as in the case of Sheba, the son of Bichri,[46] he may be delivered to them so that the others may be saved.

R. Simeon ben Lakish understands this to mean that even where one of the company had been specified by name, the others may not deliver him to the Gentiles, unless he is guilty of death as Sheba, the son of Bichri, was guilty for his rebellion against the king. R. Johanan holds that the others may save themselves by handing over the man, whose name had been specified, even if he is not guilty of death. The passage concludes with an account of a man sought by the Romans, who fled to the town of Lydda, where Joshua ben Levi resided. When the Romans besieged the town, Joshua delivered the man to them, whereupon Elijah, the prophet,

[43] Ter. VIII, 12.
[44] *Keseph Mishneh* to *Yad, Hil. Yesode Ha-Torah*, V, 5.
[45] Ter. VIII, 12 and Tos. Ter. VII, 23.
[46] II Sam. xx.

who was a regular visitant of the Rabbi, appeared to him no longer. After Joshua had fasted for many days, Elijah reappeared and rebuked him for his conduct. 'But I followed the ruling of the *Mishnah*,' objected the Rabbi. 'Yes,' replied Elijah, 'but is this a teaching that saints ought to follow (*mishnath hasidim*)?'[47]

To revert to the 'Sidney Carton' question, it is far from certain that *Ahad Ha-Am's* view is correct. There are, for one thing, references to the 'martyrs of Lydda' in Asia Minor, Lulianus and Papus, two brothers who took upon themselves the guilt for the death of the Emperor's daughter, so as to save the community as a whole.[48] It is said that in Heaven it was proclaimed that no man can stand in the celestial compartments of the martyrs of Lydda, so elevated is their station. However, it is possible, as Rav Kook suggests, that had these men not confessed, they would have been executed in any event, together with the rest of the community, for the murder of the princess.

Ahad Ha-Am assumes that Akiba's view is accepted because of the dictum that his view is always adopted if it disagrees with only one of his contemporaries. Here, too, however, Rav Kook expresses doubts.[49] In the Talmudic discussion, in which the passage from the *Siphra* is quoted,[50] it is said that R. Johanan holds that interest paid illegally by a debtor to his creditor cannot be reclaimed in court, while R. Eliezer relies on the verse: 'Take thou no usury of him, or increase; but fear thy God; that thy brother may live with thee';[51] which implies that if interest is taken, it should be returned that 'thy brother may be able to live with thee'. R. Johanan,

---

[47] For the question of the Jewish attitude towards saving the mother giving birth, at the expense of her child, see my article in the *Jewish Chronicle*: 'Mother or Baby?', Nov. 16th, 1951.

[48] Pes. 50a, Ta'an. 18b.

[49] *Mishpat Kohen* loc. cit.

[50] B.M. 62a.

[51] Lev. xxv, 36.

on the other hand, interprets the verse to agree with R. Akiba in the case of the two men and the water. From which, it would seem, that if the view of R. Eliezar is adopted, the verse cannot be interpreted to agree with Akiba, and Ben Petura's teaching would be followed. The Codes are strangely silent on the question of Akiba versus Ben Petura, but since R. Eliezar's ruling is adopted with regard to interest, the logic of the Talmudic passage quoted would demand that they follow Ben Petura; though, of course, this is no more than *pilpul* and is hardly conclusive.

But even if Akiba's view is adopted, this means no more than that there is no obligation for *both* to die, if one can drink the water and survive. In the ordinary way, this would mean that the one who has the water in his possession will drink, but this is not as *Ahad Ha-Am* says it is: 'because to preserve your own charge is a nearer duty than to preserve your neighbour's' but simply because there cannot be any *obligation* for one to hand over the water to the other, since the other would have the same obligation to hand it back again! Akiba would agree, however, that if the man holding the water wanted to give it to his neighbour, his would be a special act of piety – *middath hasiduth*. Ben Petura, too, would not object, of course, to one of the two allowing his friend to drink the water and survive. The debate between Akiba and Ben Petura concerns only the case where both want to drink; here, Akiba argues that it would be wrong for *both* to die, if one can live.

In this connection, reference should be made to a subtle distinction of *Maharam Schiff* (Meir Schiff, 1605-c.1641) in his Halakhic commentary to the Talmud. On the basis of the verse, 'because he fareth well with thee,'[52] i.e., as thine equal, the Talmud rules[53] that if the owner of a Hebrew slave has only one cushion, he must give it to the slave, for by keeping it for himself, he would not be treating the slave as an equal.

[52] Deut. xv, 16.
[53] See Tos. Kidd. 20a, s.v. *kol*.

Why, asks Schiff,[54] is the verse 'that thy brother may live *with thee*' interpreted by Akiba to mean that the man in possession of the water may keep it, while the verse 'because he is well *with thee*' is taken to mean that the owner must give up his cushion to the slave? The answer is a fairly obvious one, once it is pointed out. In the case of the water, there can be no obligation for one to hand over the water to the other, for then the other would be obliged to hand it back again. But in the case of the master and his slave, there is no such *reciprocal* obligation, for the verse 'because he is well with thee' is addressed to the master, not to the slave!

Ahad Ha-Am quotes the case of Raba mentioned above and argues that Raba would say that where the issue is saving the life of another by giving one's own life: 'Let the other be killed, and do not destroy yourself. For do what you will, a life must be lost; and how do you know that his blood is redder than yours? Perhaps yours is the redder.' This is to confuse the issue. Raba deals with murder and, as Rashi points out, it is forbidden to commit a *crime* in order to save a life, if life must be lost in committing the crime. But the sacrifice of one's life for another is no crime, for suicide is only an offence because *a* life is lost, not because *my* life is lost! Furthermore, the question of 'whose blood is redder' is irrelevant here, for it could be argued that the act of self-sacrifice in the interests of another endows the 'life' sacrificed with a significance it could not have possessed had the instinct of self-preservation prevailed.

Dr. Hertz is, of course, right that it would be an impossibility for *all* men to attempt to go through life, loving their neighbours *more* than themselves. *As thyself* is the only rule for society. But the rare individual who, in a moment of tremendous crisis, can rise to the heights of giving his life for his friend – as the Sidney Carton of fiction and the Captain Oates of fact – is a saint and would be recognised as such by Judaism. Jewish history has not lacked such 'Fools of God'.

[54] Comment. to B.M. 62a.

X

COMPASSION

THE Rabbis considered the virtue of compassion (*Raham-anuth*) to be one of the three distinguishing marks of the Jew.[1] True Israelites are 'compassionate sons of the compassionate' and he who shows no compassion demonstrates that he is not a descendant of Abraham and of those who stood at the foot of Sinai.[2] The compassionate man wins the compassion of Heaven.[3] A favourite Talmudic name for God, used particularly in the legal discussions, is *Rahamana*, 'the Compassionate'. The traditional Jewish Prayer Book contains the word for 'compassion' on page after page. One of the earliest liturgical compositions contains the petition: 'O our Father, merciful Father, the ever compassionate, have mercy upon us.'[4] Another prayer praises God for giving us in the light of His countenance 'lovingkindness and righteousness, blessing, compassion, life and peace'.[5] The Grace after Meals speaks of God feeding the whole world 'with goodness, with grace, with lovingkindness and with compassion'.[6]

The Hebrew word translated as 'compassion' in the above passages is the expressive word *Rahamim*. (Among Eastern Jews a child is frequently given the name *Rahamim*.) The word has an interesting etymology. It appears to be derived

[1] Yeb. 79a.
[2] Betz. 32b.
[3] Sabb. 151b.
[4] *Singer's Prayer Book*, p. 39.
[5] *Singer's Prayer Book*, p. 53
[6] *Singer's Prayer Book*, p. 280.

from the word *rehem*, meaning 'the womb', that is, either *'brotherly* feeling', of those born in the same womb, or *'motherly* feeling'.[7] The late Hebrew word *Rahamanuth*, describing the abstract quality, is the one most frequently used for 'compassion'. Women, say the Rabbis are particularly gifted with this quality.[8] Questions of etymology apart, the word expresses the tender feelings of a parent for his offspring. In the Bible, God's mercy and compassion are described in terms of a father's love for his children.[9]

Compassion is among the highest of the Jewish virtues, as cruelty is among the worst of the vices. The prophet Jeremiah speaks of the people from the north country who 'lay hold on bow and spear, they are cruel, and have no compassion'.[10] The prophet Amos mentions, among the nations he castigates for wanton cruelty, the people of Edom who 'did pursue his brother with the sword, and did cast off all pity, and his anger did tear perpetually, and he kept his wrath for ever'.[11] Amalek, the arch-enemy of Israel, is notorious for its cruelty.[12] The throne of God, say the Rabbis, is incomplete so long as the spirit of Amalek is abroad.[13] In Rabbinic times Amalek was identified with the barbaric German tribes, the most blood-thirsty and savage within the Roman Empire.[14]

Compassion is to be extended to the animal creation as well as to man. Though Judaism permits the taking of animal life for food and other human needs, and Jewish authorities have permitted vivisection in order to further human know-

---

[7] See B.D.B. s.v. *Rahamim.*
[8] Meg. 14b. Cf. B.B. 104b.
[9] Ps. ciii, 13, Jer. xxxi, 20.
[10] Jer. vi, 23.
[11] Amos i, 11.
[12] See article Amalek in J.E. Vol. I, p. 482.
[13] Targum Yer. to Ex. xvii, 16.
[14] Meg. 6b.

COMPASSION

ledge,[15] the causing of unnecessary suffering to animals is severely condemned.[16] The act of slaughter for food is to be carried out in as humane a manner as possible.[16a] 'A righteous man regardeth the soul of his beast.'[17] The ox was not to be muzzled while plowing[18] and an ox and an ass were not to be yoked together.[19] Before taking the eggs of fledglings from a bird's nest the mother bird was to be sent away.[20] The special greeting to one who dons a new

[15] The sources are given in H. J. Zimmels' *Magicians, Theologians and Doctors,* Lond., 1952, p. 17 and p. 177. Cf. the discussion in Morris Joseph's *Judaism as Creed and Life,* Lond., 1903, p. 477f.

[16] There are numerous references in the Rabbinic literature to the sin of causing unnecessary pain to dumb animals, e.g. B.M. 32b and freq. Cf. the Talmudic rule that one should first feed the domestic animals and then sit down to a meal, Gitt. 62a and the saying that Moses proved himself worthy of leading Israel because he had pity on the flock he tended for his father-in-law, Ex. R. II to Ex. iii, 1.

[16a] According to Maimonides, Guide III, 26 and 48 the laws of *shehitah,* ritual slaughtering, have as their purpose the avoidance of unnecessary pain.

[17] Prov. xii, 10.

[18] Deut. xxv, 4.

[19] Deut. xxii, 10.

[20] Deut. xxii, 6-7. Cf. *Mishnah* Ber. V.3 and Ber. 33b where the attempt to interpret this rule as a manifestation of God's mercy is apparently condemned. Maimonides in *Yad,* Hil. Teph. IX, 7 follows this adding that if the rule were intended as a manifestation of mercy the slaughter of animals for food would be forbidden. But in the Guide III, 48, Maimonides does interpret this rule on the grounds that the *Torah* provides that grief should not be caused to cattle or birds and that the Talmudic passage to the contrary follows the view that the precepts have no other reason but the Divine will. Cf. the statement in the *Zohar* III, 92b on the prohibition of killing an animal and its young on the same day (Lev. xxii, 28): 'Thus if a man does kindness on earth, he awakens lovingkindness above, and it rests upon that day which is crowned therewith through him. Similarly if he performs a deed of mercy, he crowns that day with mercy and it becomes his protector in the hour of need. So, too, if he

(Continued at foot of p. 138)

garment is not to be made for shoes of leather or a fur coat because these can only be obtained by the killing of an animal.[21] One of the reasons given for the prohibition of wearing shoes on the great day of *Yom Kippur* is that it is unfitting on the day in which Israel entreats God to show compassion, for Jews to wear articles of dress which have been obtained by the slaughter of animals.[22] The hunting of animals for sport is vigorously condemned by many Jewish teachers.[23] The Safed Kabbalist, Moses Cordovero, taught that man should resemble the Higher Wisdom of his Creator in refraining from doing harm to any living thing.[24] Of this mystic it is said that he would refrain from killing the gnats which stung him, or even from uprooting plants, in the belief that all things have their place in God's creation. Unlike many religious teachers, Cordovero held that man's compassion should be extended even to the wicked.[25] In this he followed the well-known Talmudic tale concerning Rabbi Meir's gifted wife, Beruria, who taught that man should pray for the death of sin, not of sinners.[26]

The Talmud tells of Rabbi Judah the Prince, the famous editor of the *Mishnah* and patriarch of his people, to whom

performs a cruel action, he has a corresponding effect on that day and impairs it, so that subsequently it becomes cruel to him and tries to destroy him, giving him measure for measure. Israel are withheld from cruelty more than all other peoples, and must not manifest any deed of the kind, since many watchful eyes are upon them,' Soncino trans., Lond. 1949, Vol. V, p. 113. On the question of the contradiction between the two passages in Maimonides see Isaac Heinemann's '*Ta'ame Ha-Mitzvoth Be-Siphroth Yisrael*', Vol. I, Jer. 1949, pp. 66-80.

[21] *Shulkhan 'Arukh 'Orah Hayyim* 243, 6.

[22] *Siddur Ha-Minhagim*, by S. Z. Schick, Munkatsch, 1884, quoted by S. J. Agnon: 'Yomin Noraim', Jer. 1956, p. 276.

[23] See Responsa *Noda Be-Yehudah*, 48.

[24] *Tomer Debhorah*, ed. Wolf Aschkenazi, Jer. 1928, end of Chapter III, p. 25.

[25] See *Tomer Debhorah* end of Chapter II, p. 22.

[26] Ber. 10a, cf. Ber. 7a.

there ran for protection a calf being led to the slaughter. 'Go,' said Rabbi Judah, 'for this you were created.' Whereupon, the legend continues, great sufferings came upon him. Some time later Rabbi Judah noticed his servant sweeping out a nest of weasels from a corner of his palace. 'Let them stay,' said the Rabbi, 'it is written: "And His tender mercies are over all His works." '[27] Upon which his sufferings left him.[28] The point of this story is that compassion is not to be fettered by cold calculation. The story is not told in support of vegetarianism. There is no suggestion that the calf should not be led to the slaughter. But the compassionate man, even when he can do nothing to prevent suffering, will have sympathy with its victims. 'Go, for this you were chosen' is the unfeeling response. This is the *motif* behind the Scriptural stories concerning righteous men pleading with God to put an end to suffering and even challenging God for allowing suffering – Abraham interceding for Sodom,[29] Moses for his people,[30] the Hasidic saint, Levi Yitzhak of Berditchev, asking God: 'What dost Thou want of Thy people Israel that they are delivered into penury and suffering?' However the burning problem of pain is grappled with, the man of faith has arrived at some understanding of why the benevolent Creator allows suffering or, at least, his reason tells him that ultimately there is no incompatibility between human suffering and God's benevolence. But such 'reasons' are for himself, when he is confronted by his own pain. So far as others are concerned 'the heart has its reasons' and compassion is stirred unhampered by attempts at theoretical justification of the existence of evil. This is the religious habit of mind in this matter as understood by Judaism. Pious resignation to the will of God is a virtue when practised on one's own behalf. It ceases to be a virtue when practised on behalf of others. There is

[27] Ps. cxlv, 9.
[28] B.M. 85a.
[29] Gen. xviii, 23-33.
[30] Ex. v, 22-23, xxxii, 11-13, Num. xiv, 13-19.

nothing heroic in being stoical concerning the sufferings of others.

But though compassion transcends reason it must be grounded in reason if it is not to degenerate into mere sentimentality. The great-hearted man is not easily swayed by caprice. Compassion is not mawkishness. There are limits to compassion. On the whole Judaism knows of two such limits. The first is with regard to justice. A judge, acting as judge, must apply the principles of the law without regard for persons. It would be as wrong for him to give a favourable judgment to a poor litigant, when the law opposes this, as it would be for him to give a favourable judgment to a rich litigant, when the law opposes it. Certainly as a man it is his duty *after* the case has been decided to help the poor but in his function as judge only the dictates of strict justice must be applied. Unless this principle is recognised, there can be no law, for the judge will be swayed by his emotions. Most civilised peoples appreciate that hard cases make bad law. In the name of compassion itself the judge must decide in accordance with justice alone, for, were the law to fail, the unjust would find no hindrance to their evil schemes. Justice must, of course, be tempered with mercy but where compassion can only be shown to a litigant at the expense of his fellow, justice and not compassion must prevail. This is implied in the remarkable Biblical verse: 'Neither shalt thou favour a poor man in his cause.'[31]

The second limit to compassion is to those who themselves lack compassion. 'He who is compassionate to the cruel,' taught one of the Rabbis 'will, in the end, be cruel to the

[31] Ex. xxiii, 3. Cf. *Mishnah*, Keth. IX, 2: 'Rabbi Akiba says: They may not show pity in a legal suit', and Sanh. 6b: 'In rendering legal judgment, David used to acquit the guiltless and condemn the guilty; but when he saw that the condemned man was poor, he helped him out of his own purse, thus executing justice and charity – justice to the one by awarding him his dues, and charity to the other by assisting him out of his own pocket.'

compassionate.'[32] For such a man's feeling does not arise from a genuine emotion of compassion but from some external whim and this is as equally likely to lead him to be cruel where compassion is needed. Judaism does not teach that all hatred is evil. The hatred of evil is a good. 'O ye that love the Lord, hate evil.'[33]

Compassion depends on imagination and lack of feeling is generally due to the lack of the ability to put oneself, in the imagination, into another's shoes. This is what Maimonides meant, and he was following earlier Jewish teachings, when he ruled that the highest degree of charity is to anticipate charity by preventing poverty.[34] Only the hard-hearted and the close-fisted remain deaf to the cry of distress calling for immediate relief. It takes a man of compassion with rarer gifts of imagination to undertake the prevention of distress. R. Hayyim Soloveitchick (d. 1918), the renowned Rabbi of Brest-Litovsk, a man whose brilliant insights into Talmudic learning were equalled only by his kindliness and generosity, once remarked of a local 'do-gooder' that he loved charity too much to be a really charitable man! There are people who so love the act of almsgiving that they would hate to see poverty abolished. But the highest aim of charity is to abolish its need. Nowadays the eighth degree of Maimonides would include working for social progress, the provision of adequate living accommodation and the abolition of slums, generous support of cancer research and of all measures which contribute to the fight against poverty, disease and squalor.

Those whom fate has treated harshly are to be the special objects of compassion. This is sound Jewish teaching. The stranger, the widow and the orphan are especially singled out

---

[32] *Yalkut,* Sam. 121 with reference to Saul who had pity on Agag (I Sam. xv, 9) but later killed the priests of Nob (I Sam. xxii, 17-19).

[33] Ps. xcvii, 10.

[34] *Yad, Hil., Matenath 'Aniyim,* X, 7.

for kindly treatment in numerous passages in the Bible.[35] The man on the bed of pain and sickness is to be visited and given words of encouragement and good cheer.[36] Mourners are to be visited and an attempt made to offer them solace and comfort.[37] It is forbidden, say the Rabbis, to suggest to those in distress that their sufferings are the result of sin.[38] This same delicacy of feeling is to be seen in the teaching that a repentant sinner should not be taunted with reminders of his past life, or a convert to Judaism from idolatry with the past of his ancestors.[39] Women are easily moved to tears and they should be spoken to in more gentle terms than those used when speaking to men. God, say the Rabbis, told Moses to speak the word of God in harsher accents to the men, in gentle accents to the women.[40] Rabbi Israel Salanter, the strict moralist whose every phrase was counted as precious and who always spoke with a great economy of words, was once observed conversing at length on all manner of frivolous topics in order to bring a little cheer into the life of a poor unfortunate. There is a Talmudic legend which tells of Elijah being asked by a Rabbi to whom he appeared which of the men then present in the market place were destined for Paradise. Elijah pointed to two jesters, men of no learning and small piety, whose great claim to immortality was that in difficult days they brought a smile to the faces of the distressed.[41] The *Hasidim* tell of one of their masters who advised a rich follower to eat and sup well. His disciples expressed astonishment that the master should show so much concern for the gratification of the rich man's appetites. The master replied: 'If this man has delicacies on his table he will be moved to care for those who have none. But if he

[35] Ex. xxii, 20-23, Lev. xix, 9-10, xxiii, 22.
[36] Ned. 39b and freq.
[37] Sot. 14a and freq.
[38] B.M. 58b.
[39] B.M. 58b.
[40] *Mekhilta* to Ex. xix, 3.
[41] Ta'an. 22a.

is satisfied with a frugal meal he will see no need for the poor man to be given more than dry bread and water.' This fellow-feeling was, in the view of the Rabbis, to be extended even to the criminal. No discrimination should be shown to the criminal after the expiation of his offence.[42] Willa Sibert Cather, the American novelist who speaks of 'pity that was for the murderer on the scaffold, as it was for the dying soldier or the martyr on the rack', was anticipated by the Rabbis who extended the Golden Rule to cover the choice of as easy a death as possible for the condemned criminal.[43] It cannot be denied that there are to be found in the Rabbinic literature references to savage methods of execution and grim modes of physical punishment as well as the rigorous exclusion of heretics from the rights and privileges of human beings, but it is almost certain that these belong to the theoretical aspects of Rabbinic justice, formulated in an age when power was no longer vested in the Jewish Courts.[44] There are few records of attempts being made to translate theory into practice.[45] In any event, the famed Talmudist and

[42] Makk. 23a.

[43] B.K. 51a, Sanh. 45a.

[44] See George Foot Moore's *Judaism*, Harvard University Press, 1927, Vol. II, p. 187f. and Louis M. Epstein: *Marriage Laws in the Bible and the Talmud*, Harvard University Press, 1942, pp. 214-215 who discusses the teachings concerning 'sectarians' – 'they are to be lowered into a pit and are not pulled out.' Epstein rightly observes: 'It is hard to tell whether these tannaitic teachings represent halakhah or preachment. If they record halakhic principles, it is surprising to find nowhere in the Talmud any practical application of them either in civil or criminal litigation. . . . These anti-sectarian statements, therefore, must be taken as propaganda material against the sects, not even intended to be formulated into law. . . .'

[45] There were exceptions in the middle ages, particularly in Spain where the Jewish Courts carried out capital punishment and even practised mutilation of criminals, a practice unknown in Talmudic times, see Salo Baron's: *The Jewish Community*, Philadelphia, 1945, Vol. II, p. 220f.

leader of Orthodox Jewry in the twentieth century, the *Hazon 'Ish,* writes in this connection that these rules are not to be applied today for nowadays religious intolerance has the effect of driving people away from religion.[46] If the character of a people can be determined by the type of enemies it makes it is to the eternal credit of the Jewish people that Israel was singled out to be the worst victim of the fiercest enemies of pity the world has known. 'Conscience,' said the Nazis, 'is a Jewish invention.' Their countryman, Nietzche, had no use for pity. Against this inhuman attitude Judaism has ever and resolutely rebelled. Judaism looks forward to the day when, in the words of the prophet,[47] the heart of stone will be changed into a heart of flesh, responsive to the call of compassion.

[46] See *Encyclopedia Talmudith,* ed. S. J. Sevin, Vol. II, Tel-Aviv, 1949, s.v. *'Epikoros,* p. 136-7.

[47] Ezek. xi, 19.

XI

TRUTH

A RABBINIC saying runs: 'The seal of the Holy One,
blessed be He, is truth.'[1] The idea appears to be, here,
that in ancient times a man would append his seal to a docu-
ment as evidence of its authenticity. This seal would bear
some distinguishing mark for identification purposes. Where
truth is found there is evidence of God's presence.[2] In the
vast Jewish literature in which the praises of truth are sung
there are references to three kinds of truthfulness (though
this classification is nowhere made explicitly): truthfulness to
God, truthfulness to one's fellow, and truthfulness to oneself.

The *motif* of speaking the truth to God is nowhere stated
more forcibly and penetratingly than in the following
Talmudic passage, one of the most remarkable in the whole
of that remarkable literature. The Men of the Great
Assembly, who flourished at the beginning of the Second
Commonwealth, reintroduced, it is said, into their prayers
the description of God as 'Mighty' and 'Awful'. These attri-
butes had been ascribed to God by Moses[3] but the prophet
Jeremiah spoke of God as 'Mighty' but not as 'Awful'.[4] For
Jeremiah argued, if aliens are destroying His Temple where

---

[1] Sabb. 55a, Yom. 69b, Sanh. 64a.
[2] But see *Rashi* ad loc. who interprets the saying to mean that God
is first, last and ever-present, just as the three letters of the
Hebrew word for truth – *'emeth* – are the first, last and middle
letters of the Hebrew alphabet – *'aleph, mem* and *tav.*
[3] Deut. x, 17.
[4] Jer. xxxii, 17f.

are His awful deeds? Daniel, who lived during the Babylonian exile, could not even speak of God as 'Mighty'[5] for he
argued, if aliens are enslaving His sons where are His mighty
deeds? But the Men of the Great Assembly 'restored the
crown to its former place'. Like Moses they felt able to speak
of God as both 'Mighty and 'Awful' for these attributes of
God are evident in the miracle of the continued existence of
the tiny nation, Israel, in spite of the attempts made by the
great world powers to destroy it. But, continues the Talmud,
if Moses had seen fit to refer to God as 'Mighty' and 'Awful'
by what right did Jeremiah and Daniel abolish something
established by the greatest of the prophets? To this R. Eliezar
(third cent.) replies: 'They knew that the Holy One, blessed
be He, is the God of truth and they could not ascribe false
things to Him.'[6] This is to say that God is worshipped in
prayer by the heart which speaks the truth it feels. There can
be no doubt that Jeremiah and Daniel *believed* that God is
Mighty and Awful but there was nothing in their experience
calculated to make this a truth felt in the heart. Their belief
was an abstract formula to which, as men of faith, they were
prepared to give assent. But such formal assent has no place
in prayer no matter how valuable it might be in religious
philosophy or apologetics. Jeremiah and Daniel. no doubt,
could have defended with great skill and eloquence the belief
in God's power and might. But for them to have uttered *in
prayer* an idea to which there was no effective response in
the heart would have been as false as a lover sending his
beloved a love poem he had copied from a book. 'A poor thing
but mine own' is the only attitude of belief worthy to be
offered by a man standing in supplication before his Maker.'[7]

The great Maimonides has an acute observation on the

---

[5] Dan ix, 4f.

[6] Yom. 69b.

[7] See Ta'an. 2a: ' "To love the Lord your God and to serve Him
with all your heart" (Deut. xi, 13). What is Service of the Heart?
You must needs say, Prayer.'

relationship between religion and inner truth. There is a Scriptural injunction according to which a good animal set aside for sacrifice must not be exchanged for one of inferior quality. Nor must an inferior animal be exchanged for a good one.[8] The first law is intelligible: only the best is good enough for God. But what reason can there be for prohibiting the exchange of a weak, puny offering for one of better quality?

Maimonides[9] offers this explanation. In a moment of intense religious enthusiasm the Israelite might set aside the best of his herd as a sacrifice; but doubts may begin to assail him when his fervour gives way to a more sober mood. He may then have misgivings about his excessive generosity. Not wishing, however, to recognise coldly calculating prudence for what it is, he may succeed in persuading himself that the inferior animal he intends to offer as a substitute, is, in some ways, at least, superior to the first. And it is to avoid this kind of dissembling that Scripture prohibits any exchange. A shrewd comment on the familiar temptation to preserve our self-respect while sacrificing our integrity by allowing faults to masquerade as virtues. Psychologists today call this 'rationalisation'. We invent reasons for doing what we want to do. At the worst level men drunk with power have used religion as a cloak to cover the most horrible and vicious deeds, not always consciously or cynically, but by permitting themselves to believe that they were serving God when they were really serving the devil.

This undeniable fact has sometimes been adduced to prove that all religion is false. But it is not religion that is at fault when base men use it to further their own ends. The Rabbis realistically faced this issue when they said that for the good man the *Torah* is a soul-healing balm, but for the depraved man the *Torah* itself becomes a deadly poison![10]

[8] Lev. xxvii, 9-10.
[9] *Yad, Hil. Temurah*, Chapter IV, 13.
[10] Yom. 72b.

True religion demands 'truth in the inward parts'.[11] Undoubtedly there are religious men whose faith is little more than an emotional prop, even a means of justifying what they know to be wrong. But the faith of the true believer is a powerful searchlight, casting its merciless beams on ignoble motives, exposing them for what they are. 'Everything in the world,' said the *Hasidic* Rabbi of Kotzk, 'can be imitated except truth. For truth that is imitated is no longer truth!'[12]

This is one of the reasons why the Freudian accusation that religion is 'wishful thinking' sounds so hollow. It is a strange wishful thinking that subjects one's deepest thoughts to the incorruptible and ever-vigilant scrutiny of the 'stern daughter of the voice of God'! Judaism, notwithstanding its refusal to dwell, as do some other faiths, on the essential sinfulness of human nature, encourages its adherents to pray at all times: 'Purify our hearts to serve Thee in truth.'[13]

It will not do, of course, to go to the opposite extreme of imagining that because human truth is often tainted that man can never arrive at the truth through the exercise of his reason. This view has won acceptance in certain theological circles. Man, it is suggested, is utterly powerless to reason about his religion and the only truths of religion he can know are those revealed to him by God's grace. It would be hard to find much support for this view in representative Jewish teaching. The obvious objection to this or any other view which denies human beings the power to think, is that it is self-stultifying. If every formulation of truth is suspect then the suspicion must extend to this formulation itself. Judaism knows full well that man can err. But Judaism has faith and confidence in man's quest for truth, from the days of the Rabbis who refused to listen to a Heavenly voice pro-

[11] Ps. li, 8.
[12] Buber: *Tales of the Hasidim: The Later Masters*, p. 284.
[13] *Singer's Prayer Book*, p. 117.

claiming those truths which it is the duty of man to discover for himself.[14]

The second aspect of truthfulness is integrity in one's dealings with others. His religion demands of the Jew that he observe the strictest standards of commercial honesty and good faith. The Bible forbids not alone direct theft but all fraudulent dealing. Oppression of others in any form, unjust weights and measures, over-reaching, are all outlawed.[15] The Rabbis extended these prohibitions. They noted, for example, that the Hebrew word for a certain measure mentioned in the Bible is *hin* – 'a just *hin*, shall ye have'.[16] This word, they connected with the word *hen*, meaning 'yes' i.e. 'thou shalt have a just "yes". Thy yea shall be just and thy nay shall be just.'[17] Cheating of any kind is forbidden, the Rabbis speak of this as 'stealing the heart'.[18] As examples of this are given: pretending that one has performed a service for another, inviting a neighbour to partake of one's hospitality knowing full well that he will refuse, and offering gifts to a friend knowing that he will not accept them.[19] This prohibition applies, like theft itself, where the victim is a Gentile as well as a Jew. In fact, in the former case the offence is greater because a 'profanation of the Name' is involved.[20] Any unfair competition in business is forbidden. Rabbi Judah (second cent.) goes so far as to forbid a shopkeeper distributing corn or nuts to children as an inducement to patronise him when their mothers send them to do the shopping. The Sages only

[14] B.M. 59b.
[15] Lev. xix, 36 and xxv, 14f., Deut. xxv, 13-16.
[16] Lev. xix, 36.
[17] B.M. 49a, cf. the comment of Abaye (ibid.) 'This means that one must not speak one thing with the mouth and another with the heart.'
[18] Hull. 94a.
[19] *Mekhilta, Mishpatim* 13, cf. *Encyclopedia Talmudith*, Vol. VI, s.v. *genebhath da'ath*, p. 225f.
[20] See *Siphra, Behar* 19, ed. Weiss, p. 110a, *Tosephta*, B.K. X, 15 and Hull, 94a.

permit this because other shopkeepers can do likewise.[21]
Utensils sold in a shop must not be camouflaged so as to
appear as new.[22] Plagiarism is frowned upon. 'He who repeats
a saying in the name of its originator,' remarked a Rabbi,
'brings redemption into the world.'[23] A man's word is sacred.
Even where there is no strict legal obligation, a man's word
should be held to be binding.[24] Even a promise which affects
no other person must be kept; a promise to abstain from
wine or food, for instance. This is the idea behind the many
laws concerning vows and their annulment. Many Rabbis
disapproved of the taking of vows even where the motive is
a sound religious one[25] but they all agree that the vow once
made must be kept. 'When a man voweth a vow unto the
Lord, or sweareth an oath to bind his soul with a bond, he
shall not break his word; he shall do according to all that
proceedeth out of his mouth.'[26]

These were not looked upon as abstract legal rules but
as the norms of daily living for Jews. Many of the Jewish
saints went to extremes in their avoidance of any semblance of
dishonesty. Of the *Haphetz Hayyim* it is told that when he
observed that more customers were frequenting his shop than
those of his competitors because of his scholarly and saintly
reputation he closed the shop each day as soon as he had
earned enough for the day's needs. The famous nineteenth
century preacher, the *Kelmer Maggid*, would buy a stamp
and tear it up whenever he sent a letter by hand for, in his
view, a failure to do this would be to cheat the postal
authorities.

The third aspect of truthfulness is being true to oneself, in

---

[21] B.M. 60a.
[22] B.M. 60a.
[23] 'Aboth, *Baraitha, Kinyan Torah,* VI, 6.
[24] *Mishnah* B.M. IV, 1 and Gem.
[25] Ned. 22a.
[26] Num. xxx, 3.

the words of the Psalmist 'speaking truth in one's heart'.[27] This involves realising the best in oneself as well as inner frankness and trustworthiness. Of a disciple of the Rabbi of Kotzk it was said that he made it a point to go to the master for the festival of Pentecost, when the Ten Commandments are read in the Synagogue, because in his home town 'Thou shalt not steal' was interpreted as 'Thou shalt not steal from others' but in Kotzk it was interpreted: 'Thou shalt not steal from thyself'! Self-delusion is a common human failing. 'Know thyself,' though the advice given by all moralists, is among the most difficult of human attainments. It may well be that no man can completely overcome the proneness to self-justification at the price of truth. But the ideal is not lost sight of in Jewish tradition. A Prayer Book rubric reads:[28] 'At all times let a man revere God in private as in public, acknowledge the truth and speak the truth in his heart.'

Here is the place to consider the 'white lie': when the truth need not be told and where even a false statement is permissible. This subject is discussed in a famous passage in the Talmud. Here it is said that if a scholar claims that an article which has been found belongs to him it may be returned to him since pious scholars do not utter falsehoods.[29] But, the Talmud goes on to say, there are three cases where even so pious a scholar is absolved from telling the truth. The three exceptions to the rule of truthfulness are given as 'tractate', 'bed', and 'hospitality'.[30] 'Tractate' is explained by the commentaries to mean that if a scholar is asked if he is familiar with a certain portion of the Talmud he may, from modesty, untruthfully say that he is ignorant. An untruth is permitted

[27] Ps. xv, 2. Cf. Makk. 24a where this verse is applied to R. Saphra to whom an offer was made while he was reciting the *Shema* and so unable to indicate his acceptance. The purchaser increased his offer but R. Saphra refused to accept more than the price he had accepted 'in his heart', cf. Hull. 94b.
[28] *Singer's Prayer Book*, p. 7.
[29] B.M. 23b-24a.
[30] B.M. ibid.

if its aim is the avoidance of a parade of learning. 'Bed' is understood by Rashi to mean that if a scholar is asked questions concerning his marital relations he may give an untruthful answer. Other commentaries remark that it is unlikely that questions of this kind would be put to a scholar by his associates and understand 'bed' to mean that if a scholar had absented himself from the House of Study because he had not yet immersed himself in a ritual bath after marital relations (as was the custom in Talmudic times) he may give some other reason for his absence.[31] According to both interpretations delicacy of feeling may prompt the telling of a 'white lie'. 'Hospitality' is understood to mean that a scholar who had been generously treated by his host may decide not to tell the truth about his reception if he fears that as a result the host may be embarrassed by unwelcome guests.[32] In addition there is the general principle of the Talmud that where peace demands it a lie may be told.[33]

The idea behind the above teaching is that though truth is important it must not be made into a fetish. Truth is a value which exists for the benefit of society and may, on occasion, be set aside if the well-being of society demands it. This idea appears to be behind the Midrashic teaching that when God was about to create man the angels formed themselves into two factions. Love said: 'Let him be created, for he will do works of love.' Truth said: 'Let him not be created, for he will practise deception.' Justice said: 'Let him be created, for he will do justice.' Peace said: 'Let him not be created, for he will be all controversy.' What did God do? He seized truth and hurled it to the earth![34] If absolute truth were always to prevail man could not endure, but the world cannot endure without truth. Consequently man must try to live by the

---

[31] Tos. B.M. ad loc. s.v. *bepuria.*
[32] B.M. ibid. Rashi s.v. *beushpiza.*
[33] Yeb. 65b.
[34] Gen. R. VIII, 5.

TRUTH

truth but there are times when truth imperils man's existence and then truth must be cast to the earth.

Truthfulness involves the repudiation of hypocrisy. The Rabbinic expression for the hypocrite is 'one whose inside is not like his outside', one who presents a front to the world that is contradicted by his inner life. The Talmud tells of the second Rabban Gamaliel (2nd cent.) who was deposed from the office of Prince because of his autocratic behaviour. Rabban Gamaliel, it is said, when in office, had issued a proclamation that any disciple whose 'inside is not like his outside' may not enter the House of Study. Under the new regime, after Rabban Gamaliel's deposition, the doorkeeper he had appointed to enforce this rule, was removed and permission was granted for all who so desired to enter. The narrative continues that on that day many new benches were added to the House of Study to accommodate the increased demand for knowledge. Rabban Gamaliel witnessing this became alarmed that by his policy of exclusion he had withheld *Torah* from Israel. Whereupon he was shown in his dreams a number of white casks full of ashes instead of wine. But the story concludes that this was shown him only to set his mind at rest.[35] The implication here is that Rabban Gamaliel's policy was in fact a mistaken one, probably because the Rabbis believed in the healing power of the *Torah* so that even the less genuine students were entitled to admission to the House of Study. But the ideal that a man's inner life should not contradict his external conduct is not lost sight of. A later teacher observed that the ark containing the *Torah* in the Sanctuary was made 'gold within and without'[36] to teach that a scholar whose 'inside is not like his outside' is no true scholar.[37] It is worthy of note that the Rabbis in their hostility to hypocrisy urge that a man's 'inside' be like his 'outside', not that his 'outside' resemble his 'inside'. It is

[35] Ber. 28a.
[36] Ex. xxv, 11.
[37] Yom. 72b.

153

generally claimed that Victorian moral and religious standards bred hypocrisy. How far this is justified is beside the point. But the Rabbis would not have approved of the twentieth century reaction to alleged Victorian hypocrisy, where hypocrisy is avoided by not even paying lip service to standards that are not observed. It is an arguable thesis that this is at least a more honest approach, but for the Rabbis the ideal was for the external pattern of good conduct to be preserved and for man's inner life to be raised to this pattern. The external behaviour of a scholar should be all that it is expected to be by convention and then hypocrisy was to be repudiated by the scholar's inner life conforming to the external pattern. His 'inside' was to be like his 'outside'!

XII

PEACE

SHALOM (peace) is one of the names of God say the Rabbis so that the traditional greeting *shalom 'alekhem,* 'peace be unto you', must not be given in the bath house where the divine name should not be uttered.[1] Both the greeting itself and the interpretation of *shalom* as God's name are the most striking evidence of the place of peace in the scale of Jewish values. The priestly blessing concludes with peace,[2] as do the Grace after Meals[3] and the most important of the prayers, the *'Amidah.*[4] The *Mishnah,* the first great Code of Jewish Law, compiled at the end of the second century, concludes with the saying of R. Simeon b. Halafta: 'The Holy One, blessed be He, found no vessel that could hold Israel's blessing excepting Peace.'[5]

To make peace between man and his neighbour or between husband and wife is one of the things 'whose fruit a man enjoys in this world while the capital is laid up for him in the world to come'.[6] A saying of the great Hillel runs: 'Be of the disciples of Aaron, loving peace and pursuing peace, loving mankind and bringing them near to the *Torah.*'[7]

Ben Zevi, the President of the State of Israel, in his Inauguration Address to the *Knesset* on 10th December, 1952 said:

[1] Sabb. 6b. Zohar III, 10b.
[2] Num. vi, 26.
[3] *Singer's Prayer Book,* p. 285.
[4] *Singer's Prayer Book,* p. 54.
[5] 'Uktz. III, 12.
[6] Pe'ah I, 1.
[7] 'Aboth I, 12.

'Peace, like charity, begins at home.' In this he was anticipated by the Rabbis who taught that if one brings peace into his home, Scripture accounts it to him as though he had brought peace to everyone in Israel; but if one brings envy and contention into his home it is as though he had brought envy and contention into Israel.[*] The first and most important contribution a man can make to the peace of the world is to create an atmosphere of peace around himself. 'You cannot find peace anywhere save in your own self,' said the *Hasidic* master Simhah Bunam of Pychyscha. Cantankerousness is frequently the manifestation of feelings of inferiority, as modern psychologists have demonstrated. The man who is unsure of himself compensates that inadequacy by asserting his superiority. With fine insight the *Besht*, the founder of the *Hasidic* movement, interpreted the verse: 'The Lord will give strength unto His people; The Lord will bless His people with peace'[*] to mean that peace is the fruit of inner strength.

Most men of good will agree on the value of peace. But what of those situations where peace conflicts with other values, particularly the value of truth? In the chapter on truth we have noted the Rabbinic views on the legitimacy of the 'white lie'. Here is the place to consider the rival claims of peace and truth. Obviously the voice of truth cannot be silenced merely on the grounds that it may disturb the peace. If a dramatic critic dislikes a play or film he owes it to his readers to state his opinion even at the risk of offending the producer and the artistes. There would be no future for book reviewing and literary standards would become non-existent if reviewers were to be inhibited by the thought that their adverse remarks might cause pain to sensitive but incompetent authors. Men of principle cannot be expected to be disloyal to their convictions because ideas can be inflammatory and provocative.

[*] ARN ed. J. Goldin, Chapter 28, Yale University Press, 1955, p. 116.
[*] Ps. xxix, 11.

PEACE

This problem was not evaded by the Rabbis, who recognised the value of the 'controversy for the sake of Heaven'.[10] Generally, Rabbinic teaching approves of a lie whose purpose is to promote peace.[11] And yet the Rabbinic literature abounds in vehement discussions on matters of law, philosophy, morals and religion. The contradiction is easily resolved. Where no important principle is at stake the Rabbis prefer peace to truth. Tactfulness is not a discovery of the twentieth century. But, where principle is involved, truth must be preferred to peace, or, as the Rabbis put it, adherence to truth in obedience to principle results in peace.[12] The operative expression is 'for the sake of Heaven'. The most impassioned quarrels have their place in human life if they are the result of the firm adherence to the respective facets of truth of the verbal duellists. The rival schools of Hillel and Shammai are given as the example of those who engage in controversy not from personal animosity but for the sake of Heaven.[13] These schools debated hundreds of important religious matters[14] (with the danger, observes the Talmud,[14a] of the *Torah* becoming 'two *Toroth*') yet they set the pattern for the future discussions of Judaism. Though, occasionally, one finds in the Talmud a nostalgia for the good old days when 'there was no controversy in Israel'[15] the Talmud has become the work second only to the Bible as the authority for

[10] 'Any controversy that is for the sake of Heaven shall in the end be of lasting worth, but any that is not for the sake of Heaven shall not in the end be of lasting worth' ('Aboth V, 17).

[11] 'One may modify a statement in the interests of peace' (Yeb. 65b).

[12] 'Said R. Hiyya by Abba: Even father and son, master and disciple, who study *Torah* at the same gate become enemies of each other; yet they do not stir from there until they come to love each other' (Kidd. 30b).

[13] 'Aboth ibid.

[14] A full list of these is given in I. H. Weiss's *Dor*, Vol. I, Chapter 19, p. 177f.

[14a] Tos. Hag. II, 9, Sanh. 88b, Sot. 47b.

[15] Tos. Hag. Sanh. and Sot. ibid.

Judaism, partly, at least, because of its non-monolithic character, the consequence of differing views being recorded and respected. The man of principle and courage is not averse to a good fight in a good cause and he need not be deprived of it in the name of peace. There is a darker side to religious controversy as we all appreciate today. But it would be a sad day for religion if men could never feel deeply on the issues it raises. 'Cakes and ale' are not the only things the virtuous are not called upon to reject.

That war is a great evil is underlined on many pages of Jewish teaching. Although the Bible appears to sanction war, it requires little reflection to recognise that the Biblical ideal is the total abolition of war. (For that matter the Bible appears to recognise slavery but in reality the slavery laws were clearly intended to mitigate the severities of this ancient and deep-rooted institution. In ancient times it was impossible for the Bible to ordain its complete cessation. Ancient Society was based on slavery and there were sound social and political reasons for its retention. But the spirit of the *Torah* was definitely opposed to slavery so that we cannot doubt that its final abolition in Western lands was a fulfilment of the *Torah*.) So it is with war. Judaism looks forward to the time when the dream of the prophets will be realised: 'And they shall beat their swords into plowshares, and their spears into pruning-hooks; nation shall not lift up sword against nation, neither shall they learn war any more.'[16] The *Mishnah*[17] tells us that when R. Eliezar (early second century) ruled that a man may go out on the Sabbath with a sword, bow, club, shield or spear, because these are 'adornments' and cannot be considered a 'burden', the Sages objected: 'They are naught but a reproach,' quoting in support the verse from Isaiah. The Book of Chronicles states that David was not allowed to build the Temple because he engaged in much warfare: 'Thou hast shed blood abundantly, and hast made

[16] Is. ii, 4.
[17] Sabb. VI, 4.

great wars; thou shalt not build a house unto My name, because thou hast shed much blood upon the earth in My sight."[18] The *Mekhilta*, one of the oldest Rabbinic commentaries on the Bible, explains the Biblical law forbidding the use of iron on the stones of the altar,[19] because it is unfitting for that which shortens the life of man (iron from which weapons of war are fashioned) to be used on that which prolongs his life (the altar, through which he entreats his Maker). 'And it follows,' continues the *Mekhilta*, 'that if stones that can neither hear nor speak yet because they promote peace between Israel and their Father in Heaven, the Holy One, blessed be He, said "thou shalt not build it of hewn stones," then he who makes peace between city and city, between people and people, between government and government, will certainly be spared from suffering.'[20]

This is the ideal. But in a world from which war has not as yet been abolished, Judaism recognises the realities of the situation and legislates accordingly. Consequently, Judaism has much to say on problems to which warfare gives rise. It is clear that Judaism does not call for a policy of passive non-resistance when a nation is attacked. A war of defence is not only permitted but is advocated. The authorities quote in this connection the famous Talmudic maxim: 'If one comes to slay thee, forestall by slaying him.'[21] (But if this is the justification for a war of defence it would seem to rule out the use of nuclear weapons in defence because the probable consequences of the use of these weapons would be to wipe out the larger portion of the whole human race, including the defenders. The Rabbis would say that if a man tries to kill you you may kill him *in order to save yourself*. There is no suggestion that you may kill both him and yourself because he attacked you.) Furthermore it is the duty of other

[18] I Chron. xxii, 8.
[19] Ex. xx, 22.
[20] Mekhilta to Ex. loc. cit.
[21] Sanh. 72a, cf. S. Sevin: *'Le-'or Ha-Halakhah'*, p. 5f.

nations to support the nation attacked. The verse: 'Whoso sheddeth man's blood by man shall his blood be shed,'[22] means, according to one interpretation, that 'the blood of the pursued be saved by the blood of the pursuer'.[23] It is a duty to save the life of an intended victim of homicide, even if this necessitates the slaying of the would-be murderer.

It is relevant here to quote a brilliant interpretation of an ancient Rabbinic law by the late Rav Kook concerning warfare. We read in the book of Deuteronomy:

> And it shall be, when ye draw nigh unto the battle, that the priest shall approach and speak unto the people, and shall say unto them: Hear, O Israel, ye draw nigh this day unto battle against your enemies; let not your heart faint; fear not, nor be alarmed, neither be ye affrighted at them; for the Lord your God is He that goeth with you, to fight for you against your enemies, to save you.[24]

The priest who performed this function is known in the Talmudic literature as the *mashuah milhamah* ('the annointed for war'). According to Rabbinic ruling his post, unlike that of the king or high priest, was not a hereditary one.[25] Why should this position not be handed down from father to son? Rav Kook gives this explanation. The idea of a hereditary position is to express permanence in human affairs. But peace is the only natural state for mankind, it is the only state deserving of permanence. War, on the other hand, is always, at the best, a necessary evil; it has no permanence, it is unnatural to man. Consequently, there can be no question of a hereditary appointment for a functionary connected with warfare, but only for one who operates in times of peace.

[22] Gen. ix, 6.
[23] Sanh. 72b.
[24] Deut. xx, 2-4.
[25] Yom. 72b, see Sevin op. cit. pp. 27-28.